WITHDRAWN

Clinical Practice in Adoption

Pergamon Titles of Related Interest

Bornstein/Bornstein MARITAL THERAPY:
A Behavioral-Communications Approach

Brassard/Germain/Hart PSYCHOLOGICAL MALTREATMENT
OF CHILDREN AND YOUTH

Plas SYSTEMS PSYCHOLOGY IN THE SCHOOLS

Roberts PEDIATRIC PSYCHOLOGY: Psychological Interventions
and Strategies for Pediatric Problems

Related Journals*

CHILD ABUSE AND NEGLECT

CHILDREN AND YOUTH SERVICES REVIEW

CLINICAL PSYCHOLOGY REVIEW

JOURNAL OF CHILD PSYCHOLOGY AND PSYCHIATRY
AND ALLIED DISCIPLINES

JOURNAL OF SCHOOL PSYCHOLOGY

*Free sample copies available upon request

PSYCHOLOGY PRACTITIONER GUIDEBOOKS
EDITORS
Arnold P. Goldstein, Syracuse University
Leonard Krasner, Stanford University & SUNY at Stony Brook
Sol L. Garfield, Washington University in St. Louis

Clinical Practice in Adoption

ROBIN C. WINKLER
University of Western Australia
Perth, Australia

DIRCK W. BROWN
Orient, NY

MARGARET VAN KEPPEL
Perth, Australia

AMY BLANCHARD
San Carlos, CA

KIRTLEY LIBRARY
COLUMBIA COLLEGE
COLUMBIA, MO 65216

PERGAMON PRESS
New York · Oxford · Beijing · Frankfurt
São Paulo · Sydney · Tokyo · Toronto

U.S.A.	Pergamon Press, Inc., Maxwell House, Fairview Park, Elmsford, New York 10523, U.S.A.
U.K.	Pergamon Press plc, Headington Hill Hall, Oxford OX3 0BW, England
PEOPLE'S REPUBLIC OF CHINA	Pergamon Press, Room 4037, Qianmen Hotel, Beijing, People's Republic of China
FEDERAL REPUBLIC OF GERMANY	Pergamon Press GmbH, Hammerweg 6, D-6242 Kronberg, Federal Republic of Germany
BRAZIL	Pergamon Editora Ltda, Rua Eça de Queiros, 346, CEP 04011, Paraiso, São Paulo, Brazil
AUSTRALIA	Pergamon Press Australia Pty Ltd., P.O. Box 544, Potts Point, N.S.W. 2011, Australia
JAPAN	Pergamon Press, 5th Floor, Matsuoka Central Building, 1-7-1 Nishishinjuku, Shinjuku-ku, Tokyo 160, Japan
CANADA	Pergamon Press Canada Ltd., Suite No. 271, 253 College Street, Toronto, Ontario, Canada M5T 1R5

Copyright © 1988 Pergamon Books, Inc.

All Rights Reserved. No part of this publication may be reproduced, stored in a retrieval system or transmitted in any form or by any means: electronic, electrostatic, magnetic tape, mechanical, photocopying, recording or otherwise, without permission in writing from the publishers.

First edition 1988

Library of Congress Cataloging in Publication Data
Clinical practice in adoption/Robin C. Winkler . . . [et al.].
p. cm. -- (Psychology practitioner guidebooks)
Bibliography: p.
Includes index.
ISBN 0-08-034222-1 : $22.50 (est.). ISBN 0-08-034221-3 (pbk.) : $12.95 (est.)
1. Adoption-Psychological aspects. 2. Clinical psychology.
I. Winkler, Robin. II. Series.
RC455.4.A35C58 1988
155.4'45-dc19   88-2659

British Library Cataloguing in Publication Data
Clinical practice in adoption. — (Psychology practitioner guidebooks).
1. Children. Adoption
I. Winkler, Robin C. II. Series
362.7'34
ISBN 0-08-034222-1 Hardcover
ISBN 0-08-034221-3 Flexicover

Printed in Great Britain by A. Wheaton & Co. Ltd., Exeter

To the memory of
Robin C. Winkler

Contents

Foreword	ix
Preface	xi
Acknowledgements	xiii
Introduction	xv
1. THE CHANGING FOCUS OF ADOPTION	1
2. DELIVERY OF POST ADOPTION SERVICES	22
3. BASIC CLINICAL ISSUES	30
4. BIRTH PARENTS	48
5. ADOPTIVE PARENTS	69
6. THE ADOPTEE	85
7. SPECIAL ISSUES IN ADOPTION	100
8. THE FUTURE	119

References 121

Suggested Readings 124

Glossary of Terms and Phrases 126

Author Index 129

Subject Index 131

About the Authors 135

Psychology Practitioner Guidebooks 136

Foreword

The authors have provided a long overdue and much needed work. Despite the fact that an increasing number of books on the subject of adoption have been published within the last decade, none has specifically addressed the issue of clinical treatment. Finally we have such a book, written by four well-qualified professionals.

Geographically, the world of adoption covers most of our planet and finds inhabitants in all countries. Regardless of cultural differences, members of the adoption community share universal needs and feelings. The authors of this book come from two continents far apart from each other. Though distant in miles, they are, nevertheless, close and connected by their intense concern and involvement in the adoption movement.

The adoption movement is a loosely constructed non-structured federation of organizations, self-help groups, search groups, discussion groups, professionals, paraprofessionals, and non-aligned members of the triangle. It is really only during the past decade that we have seen the adoption movement grow and profoundly influence practices within the institution of adoption. Revolutionary change has come about in our understanding and acceptance of the lifelong process that adoption represents for all of the members of the triangle: birth parents, adoptees, and adoptive parents. Secrecy, anonymity, and high walls of separation are no long guaranteed — or even considered desirable — by adoption agencies and their staffs. Adoptive placements today are more open, with potential contact available on behalf of the child. Searches may become unnecessary in the future because adoptees and birth parents will all know one another, or know where to find one another.

A great deal has been accomplished in one short ten-year period, and the birth parents, adoptees, adoptive parents, and professionals who have worked so hard have every right to feel proud of their achievements on behalf of future adoptive placements. They also deserve our thanks for teaching adoptees and birth parents how to search and effect reunions. What was once a totally frustrating and impossible task is now at least within the realm of possibility, legal or underground. A relatively small but devoted group of people has built a movement that, despite difficulties, is strong and cohesive. We all care about each other and cooperate willingly. It is for this writer a pleasure to know people like the authors of this book, to meet them at conferences, to ask them to help, and to be asked by them for assistance.

What has been missing is the organized, structured, recorded knowledge of how to treat those members of our current client/patient population who have specific problems resulting from membership in the adoption family. We have identified problem areas, even given them names and descriptions. We have outlined the need for post-adoption services, and succeeded in establishing such units in many different communities. Many of these post-adoption services have been in the unfortunate and unnecessary position of "recreating the wheel" because no guidelines existed. Even worse, most of the mental health practitioners in the various disciplines know virtually nothing about adoption-related problems. They tend to minimize or ignore the importance of that area, to the detriment of successful treatment. Numerous self-help groups have evolved as part of the adoption movement, and members could certainly benefit from reading and discussing books that address their issues.

Finally, in answer to these needs, the first comprehensive book to help interested parties learn about clinical practice in adoption. The authors have accomplished a monumental task, surveying the field of adoption and focusing on multiple areas, each with sensitivity and understanding. They accept the reader, regardless of orientation, as a participant in the discovery and evaluation of adoption issues. Treatment is not seen as needed in sickness or pathology only. Treatment is seen as preventative, educational, exploratory, and available in many different modalities.

For me, this book has special value. I know two of the authors personally and I respect all of them greatly. I agree with their approach and find their basic foundation to be strong and sound. I find their writing to be clear, simply worded, logical, and most important, interesting. The innate compassion and warmth of the authors comes through loudly and clearly. They care about birth parents, adoptees, adoptive parents, and even social workers and mental health practitioners. They are part of this world on both a professional and personal level. They know the people they are writing about, and they offer us that same opportunity to know them and to be able to help more effectively. This is a book to be read, reread, and referred to many, many times.

Annette Baran, MSW, LCSW
Co-author, *Adoption Triangle* (Anchor, New York, 1978)
and *Lethal Secrets* (Dodd, Mead, New York, 1988)

Preface

The guiding spirit behind this book is Robin Winkler and it is to Robin that we dedicate this book. While a visiting professor of Psychology at Stanford University in the spring of 1985, Robin invited Dirck Brown to collaborate with him in writing this book. They later asked Margaret van Keppel and Amy Blanchard to join their writing team.

To our great sorrow, Robin Winkler died in Perth, Australia at the age of 41 on November 26, 1986, after a long illness. An Associate Professor of Psychology at the University of Western Australia, Robin began his career at the University of New South Wales and at the State University of New York at Stony Brook. He later held visiting appointments at Stanford University, Texas A & M University, and the University of Thessaloniki. He took up his appointment at the University of Western Australia in 1976. Robin's heavy involvement with the area of adoption began in early 1981. He soon recognized that there was almost no knowledge base in this area and that the adoption experience was not only misunderstood but filled with myths. With these insights, Robin began to pursue this area of inquiry with enormous energy and commitment for the next six years of his life — even during his long period of ill health.

Robin's work reflected his commitment to the pursuit of sound knowledge, just and humane adoption laws and practices, the involvement of all those personally touched by the adoption experience, and much-needed legislative reform. As a result of his spirit of innovation and creative research, he established the Adoption Research and Counseling Service at the University of Western Australia — the first independent, post-adoption counseling and research service in Australia and, to our knowledge, the first university-based service of this kind in the world.

Robin carried his message to community and professional groups throughout Australia and the United States. His efforts served to do much to demythologize the adoption experience, improve practice, and empower members of the adoption triad and their extended families.

As founding chair of the Western Australia Committee on Adoption and Alternative Families, he created a powerful group for the reform of adoption laws and practice in that part of the world. For Robin, the adoption experience was more than an area of inquiry and practice — it was an integral part of his life as he exercised his special research and clinical skills. His work in adoption gave full expression to his enormous energy and drive — more than that, it gave expression to his lifelong commitment to justice and human dignity and his love for people.

While living in Palo Alto, California, Dirck Brown founded and became the first executive director of the Post Adoption Center for Education and Research (PACER). Under his leadership, beginning in 1979, PACER became a community based non-profit center, concerned with the education of lay persons and professionals regarding the lifelong nature of the adoption experience for all members of the adoption triad and their families. PACER served as a model organization in its emphasis on the need for education and support activities, all of which are equally welcoming to all members of the adoption triad. Dirck's conviction then and now is that programs and services need to be developed which are a contemporary response to the increasingly complex social and human concerns surrounding the adoption experience.

As a therapist in Orient, New York, Dirck continues to be involved in the adoption arena through writing and conducting conferences and workshops, as well as serving on the board of directors of the American Adoption Congress.

Margaret van Keppel is a clinical psychologist in Perth, Australia. She and Robin Winkler worked collaboratively from 1981 to the time of Robin's death in November 1986. Together they conducted a national research study, "Relinquishing Mothers in Adoption, Their Long Term Adjustment," published by the Australian Institute of Family Studies in 1984. Margaret was on the staff of the University of Western Australia's Adoption Research and Counseling Service until September 1985. She now works at the Centrecare Marriage and Family Service in Perth. Her post-adoption work includes counseling, consultation, training, and lobbying for adoption reform. In 1986, Margaret was awarded the West Australian Women's Fellowship, which enabled her to travel abroad to study post-adoption services.

Amy Blanchard is a clinical psychologist in private practice in San Jose, California. She met Dirck Brown while conducting her dissertation research on birth mothers, and later served on the board of directors of PACER. She has special interest in clinical work with members of the adoption community. Her dissertation, "Birth Mothers Who Search: An Exploratory Study," substantially extended our knowledge base of the birth mother experience and motivation to search.

Acknowledgements

We are indebted to friends and loved ones who provided us with support, guidance, and editorial assistance throughout the preparation of the manuscript — Molly Brown, Jeanne Brown, Janet Davies, Walter Horeb, Ruth and Dun Sherer, and Joe Davis.

Margaret's contribution to the book, in the later stages, was enhanced by the knowledge she gained while traveling under the auspices of the 1986 Western Australian Women's Fellowship.

Margaret and Robin's colleague, Sue Midford, is acknowledged for her thoughtful, unique, and incisive contributions during the periods when they worked closely together. The fruits of their labors, as well as the hours spent discussing clinical issues in post adoption, are reflected in this book.

Emma May Vilardi, founder and president of the International Soundex Reunion Registry in Carson City, Nevada, pioneered many of the ideas and concerns of this book long before they were realized by all of us.

We are indebted to our clients over the years and the members of the adoption triad with whom we have worked for teaching us what we know. We hope that we have done justice to their experiences.

Introduction

This book has been written for three main groups of readers: clinicians from a range of disciplines (psychology, social work, psychiatry, counseling); facilitators of adoption-related self-help groups; and specialist adoption (including post-adoption) workers. It may also be of interest and benefit to members of the adoption triad. Its aims are threefold as well. First, we aim to provide a comprehensive knowledge base for those working in many different settings, providing services to members of the adoption triad; second, to develop the skills of such workers; and third, in so doing to improve the quality of life for all those affected by an adoption experience, in the past, present, and future.

THE PROBLEMS

Estimates are that one in 15 persons are personally affected by an adoption experience. Adoption is a life-course issue which affects adoptees, adoptive parents, and birth parents, as well as the families of each of these three parties — all of which make up the extended adoption family.

Clinicians see many people affected by adoption, and yet have little specialized knowledge about how to handle the adoption aspects of their client's problems. Therefore, more often than not, (in the experience of the authors' clients in specialist post-adoption services) the *clients* adoption experience has been ignored, minimized, or misunderstood by their therapist or counselor. Professionals generally do not know how to handle adoption-related problems except by denying the significance of adoption or by responding to stereotypes.

Specialist adoption practice has focused primarily on the period in which infants or children are relinquished and then adopted; in fact, adoption is a *life-course process*, which unfolds over each person's life. Professional adoption specialists do not have the training to provide services over the full life course of adoption, yet are increasingly being asked to provide such services.

There is evidence that members of the adoption triad constitute a high risk group for behavioral, emotional, or relationship problems; therefore, they have a special need for effective, appropriate services.

Because adoption has been seen as an event rather than a process, these problems are often poorly dealt with by adoption workers. Therefore, there is a special need for clinical skills in both adoption specialists and general clinicians to deal with adoption-related problems. There is also a major unmet need for post-adoption service structures in which these skills are fostered.

Recent developments make this an area of special concern. These developments include the increased adoption rate of previously hard-to-place children; increased cross-racial adoption; the greater willingness of birth mothers to talk about the long-term emotional cost of relinquishment; the greater willingness of adoptees to actively consider search and reunion; and the "coming out" of adoptive parents who previously may have not wished to talk about their "difference" from other families.

A large number of self-help organizations have formed around these issues. Such organizations provide counseling services (both informally and formally), but these services are frequently staffed by insufficiently trained and supported volunteers. They need a practical handbook to guide their work and warn them of problem areas.

THE SCOPE OF THIS BOOK

Chapter 1 introduces the reader to the life-course perspective of the adoption experience for all members of the extended adoption family, and places that experience in the appropriate social/historical context. In chapter 1, we also review, both philosophically and functionally, recent developments in adoption, and their significance for the practicing clinician.

Chapter 2 is an overview of the delivery of post-adoption services and programs. Both professional services and those conducted by self-help organizations are described in some detail, with emphasis on the importance of collaboration between the various sectors of service.

Chapter 3 presents clinical issues, assessment procedures, history taking, and other intake procedures; the use of such tools as the genogram; how to distinguish clinical issues which may be adoption related from those which are not; self-assessment by the clinician; and the issues presented when the clinician is himself or herself a member of an adoption triad.

Chapter 4 focuses on the birth parent experience from the life course perspective, including the decision-making (pre-relinquishment) period, problems of the immediate post-relinquishment period, and problems in later life. Suggestions follow as to how these problems can be handled in clinical practice.

Chapter 5 is concerned with the adoptive parent experience. The major issues facing adoptive parents are presented, both in terms of pre- and post-adoption and in relation to their child's developmental stages from infancy to adulthood.

In Chapter 6, we describe the adoptee's experience: the special issues facing the adolescent adoptee, the process of search and reunion, and the continuing clinical issues the adoptee can present. Case studies are presented in chapters four, five, and six.

Chapter 7 is concerned with special issues — "special needs adoption", surrogacy, artificial insemination by donor (AID), transracial adoption, and "open adoption."

Chapter 8 presents issues we believe to be significant as we look into the future — what special new developments are likely to face clinicians and other service providers and the adoption community in the years immediately ahead.

Chapter 1
The Changing Focus of Adoption

The focus of clinical practice in adoption has, until recently, been the placement of babies and young children with adoptive parents. This focus is in response to the several needs of the children, the needs of the parents wanting children, and the need for disadvantaged children to be raised in caring families, rather than in institutions.

Once the child and adoptive parents are brought together, adoption services have tended to grind to a halt. It is as though adoption is no longer of concern to the child as the child grows into an adult, to the adoptive parents who struggle to parent well over the years, and to the birth parents who relinquished a child whom they will probably never see again.

The cloud that falls over the life course development of all those involved in an adoption is formed from several sources. Adoptive parents have wanted to raise their adopted child in the same way as they would raise (or do raise) a child of their own creation. Adoptees have been kept in the dark about their origins and have been uncertain, as have their adoptive parents, as to how much the problems they may encounter are a result of having been adopted or might simply have occurred anyway. Birth parents were advised to put their troubles behind them and get on with the rest of their lives. This silence about the subsequent lives of those affected by an adoption placement has affected the helping professions.

THE NEED FOR THIS BOOK

This book focuses primarily on the needs of those affected by the adoption experience as it has been largely practiced; i.e., the placement of infants, born to young unwed parents, with adoptive parents who have shared similar cultural and racial background.

Adoptees, adoptive parents, and birth parents make up what we refer to here as the extended adoption family. For every adoption, there is an extended adoption family, the members of which deal with adoption as a contemporary issue in their lives for many years after an initial placement. As we shall see, there are many difficulties arising from adoption, which affect all members of this extended adoption family in different ways. Where can help be sought with these problems? If help is sought from a general health professional (psychiatrist, clinical psychologist, social worker), the health professional who has little specialized knowledge about adoption is also faced with the question, "Is this an adoption-related problem or is it not?" If the client feels it is, is adoption being used as an excuse or as a mechanism to hide the "real" source of the problem? If the professional feels it is adoption-related but the client does not, how can this impasse be broken? If both agree to work on adoption-related aspects, how should this work proceed? These are some of the questions we shall address in the book.

Members of the extended adoption family frequently, however, find themselves dissatisfied with the lack of sensitivity among generalist professionals, and seek support from the many self-help organizations that have developed to fill the service vacuum in this area. There are now thousands of such self-help organizations around the world, struggling to lift the clouds that have enveloped the adult lives of the extended adoption family. These self-help organizations provide extremely important counseling and support services. Their staff are usually untrained volunteers, albeit often experienced. They have little in the way of professional support to help them in their counseling and to deal with complex cases. Frequently, their lobbying efforts prevent them from providing adequate counseling services. This book is designed to assist them in their work.

On the whole, members of the adoption family tend not to return for help to the original agency that arranged the adoption placement, particularly if many years have passed since the original placement. This is so for several reasons. The agency is part of a distant past. The birth parents often have only a hazy memory of the agency, and the memories are frequently painful. The adoptive parents had to be put through a difficult assessment period prior to receiving a child. The adoptee, of course, unless placed as an older child, has no memories at all of the agency. If placed as an older child, the adoptee is also likely to have painful memories. Many adoption agencies, however, have begun to recognize the limitations of past practices and are developing post-adoption services. It is also for these adoption specialists, those who have shifted their focus, that this book is written.

However, this book is ultimately for the well-being of the extended adoption family itself.

The scope of the problem

Because we place adoption in the context of life-course development, we deal with the impact of past adoption placements on contemporary experience. To estimate the size of the problem we are dealing with, we therefore must consider not only the *present rate* of adoption placements, but also the *past rates*. This is crucial since, in many countries, the past rates of adoption are much higher than present rates. Our research and clinical experience shows clearly that adoption-related issues can remain "hot" and pressing right across the lifespan. This accumulated impact is given particular weight through the force of social history. Many older adoption practices were cruel and insensitive, reflecting older, harsher social attitudes; the scars left by these practices have never really healed for many people. The probability, therefore, is substantial that adoption-related problems will occur over a person's full life course.

Further, these rates need to be considered in a systems or transactional context. Adoption is inherently about relationships, both real and fantasied: relationships between adoptee and adoptive parents, adoptee and birth parents, and adoptive parents and birth parents. A secondary but crucial set of relationships involve the impact of this first set upon the adoptee's subsequent own family, the birth mother's subsequent own family, and the adoptive parent's biological children. Adoption issues reverberate through the extended adoption family system in complex ways. They do so in a particularly subtle way, frequently clouded by secrecy and half-suspected truths or fears, and accumulating layer upon layer of meaning as time passes with family history.

It is usual, however, to multiply numbers of past adoptions within the immediately past generation and multiply them by five (the two adoptive parents, the two birth parents, and the adoptee), to obtain an estimate of the number of people affected by adoption. The result of this simple calculation (usually confused by poor regionally based and insufficient record systems) is staggering. In Western countries it is conservatively estimated that one in fifteen people are personally affected by adoption.

Unfortunately we cannot so easily make the next step of estimating what the probabilities are of those one in 15 experiencing difficulties arising from adoption. This largely reflects the paucity of research on adoption as a life-course development issue. We shall see, however, that present indications are that adoption constitutes a significant risk factor in several ways. We shall see that adoptees appear to be over-represented in children's clinics (although this evidence is far from clear); that adoptee identity issues can be particularly problematic; that birth mothers can experience a deep, debilitating, and growing sense of loss for many years after relinquishment; that adoptive parents face special difficulties in parenting; and that relationships within and between the subsystems of the extended adoption family can be emotionally crippling. These particular kinds of difficulties and others will each be considered separately in their turn.

It is not our intention to engage in debates over whether the institution of adoption itself is a good or bad thing. This is beyond our scope. Inevitably, by focusing on problems that arise with adoption, an impression might be given that the best form of prevention in this area is to eliminate adoption. Many have been led to this conclusion, arguing for alternative forms of family building and permanent care for children — for example, guardianship, custody. or fostering. Others respond by calling for better current adoption placement procedures, in order to benefit from the experience gained from understanding post-adoption problems. Still others have a third kind of emphasis, emphasizing not so much abolition or better service procedures but changes in adoption legislation. We shall, of course, touch upon these issues because they are unavoidable, but we shall attempt to restrict ourselves to immediate clinical concerns. Each of the authors has been involved in policy debates, legislative issues, and all that such involvement entails.

Our clinical experiences in two countries, so distant from each other, have drawn us to the same conclusions: members of the extended adoption family typically find themselves experiencing similar kinds of problems, and have difficulty in finding a suitable person or agency who can assist them with their problems. There are simply insufficient numbers of sensitive, experienced practitioners or service systems in the post-adoption area.

PATHWAYS TO THE CLINICIAN

The following statements illustrate some of the clinical issues common to the adoption experience:

1. "Is what I am experiencing really related to adoption or am I using adoption as an excuse or crutch, a defense?"
2. "My life seemed to be going along steadily — adoption just wasn't an issue for me. Then I found out I was adopted; my first child was born; I divorced .... suddenly I found myself plunged into crisis."
3. "I feel so alone, confused and bewildered about this. My family and friends don't understand because they have not experienced adoption and I don't know anyone else in a similar situation."
4. "I went to see a therapist but she didn't know anything about adoption. She kept trying to turn my experience into something else and somehow I didn't feel this was right. I just stopped going and felt even more alone."
5. "After lots of hesitation, I finally contacted a self-help group. It was a relief to hear about others but after a while I found they were so focused on issues like search or lobbying that there was no chance for me to really talk."
6. "I have been to workshops and talks but I think I need something more.

There are many scary areas I know I need to go into and I need some expert help, but whom can I trust."
7. "I've gone along with all this new adoption talk and now find things have gotten worse rather than better."

Several themes run through these statements. The theme which suffuses the whole field is the experience of alienation that springs from the absence of public awareness about post-adoption issues. Also common is the experience, at the end of a long and emotional day of sharing experiences, of saying with relief and happiness: "I never knew who I was before today. Today I found myself. Thank you all". This conspiracy of silence about post-adoption experience has been breaking down over the last decade, although such openness has still to be felt in many quarters. It is therefore timely, although also overdue, for guides to appear on clinical practice for post-adoption problems.

Another theme reflects not only a reluctance to speak due to social constraints but a reluctance based on personal defensiveness. Over the years, adoption issues, though present, have been covered over through fear and hostility — fear of rejection, of finding out, of the consequences of facing up, of interference from a loved one; hostility about betrayals and rejections, either imagined or real, about treatment from others.

Frequently, a lifetime has been built upon secrets, and mysteries, and imagined figures from the past which have become encrusted with romance and tragedy. Such habits of personal and family survival, habits of a lifetime, prevent adoption clients from coming forward for help more than other clients. The weight of complex family histories is particularly heavy.

Yet another theme is secrecy and illusion. Whole lives can be built upon premises that are suddenly found to be false, — e.g., when an adult adoptee discovers he is adopted. Adoptive parents may have built their families around the illusion that their family is no different and find themselves bewildered by a confused, rejecting adolescent adoptee who seems to want now to reject the love and caring in which they have invested so much. Birth parents who thought relinquishment was well behind them discover suddenly, on a birthday or death, that it is not, and slowly come to recognize that an issue long thought away and gone is in fact still very present and close.

THE SPECIAL ROLE OF SELF-HELP ORGANIZATIONS

Self-help adoption organizations are very familiar with these experiences. As is too often the case, self-help organizations have generally responded to the need for better services, policies, and laws in advance of professionally based structures. A time-honored role for self-help organizations is to increase public and professional awareness of its members' experiences and to provide their own services where none have been before. There are now several major international and national self-help organizations, such as Adoption Jigsaw, groups affiliated with the American Adoption Congress, the International Soundex Reunion Registry, and the Adoptee Liberty Movement Association (ALMA), which conduct telephone counseling, search and support services, legislative advocacy, and regular meetings. However, they rarely have ongoing clinical support services (although we shall consider exceptions to this general rule).

Part of our concern here will be to encourage the integration of clinical support sources, professional and self-help. This we wish to do in several ways by:
- developing the skills and availability of professionals to whom referrals can be made;
- developing the skills of self-help workers so that they can expand their services;
- promoting new structures in self-help organizations.

To do this, however, requires that self-help organizations face squarely an issue that all self-help groups are eventually forced to face: How much time, effort and money do they have available to put into social and community action (lobbying, promoting search, etc.), and how much into supporting individuals in difficulty?

Obviously our focus here will be more on the latter given the nature of this book. The ongoing dilemma for self-help groups is to strike the best balance possible between support needs and lobbying needs. When a balance is not reached, personal difficulties become entrenched as organizational difficulties.

THE LARGER ADOPTION COMMUNITY

An article of faith throughout our clinical work has been that just as there is an extended adoption family, there is an adoption community. This community is made up of self-help organizations, professionals and professionally based organizations, government agencies, interested legislators, and the extended adoption families themselves. We have chosen to write about clinical services for adoption in ways that are sensitive to this adoption community and not just to the immediate clients. Because of the nature of post-adoption problems, case management so often entails working with multiple agencies. Yet the adoption community is frequently fragmented and in conflict. Professional and self-help organizations often distrust each other, different self help organizations often find it difficult to work together, and policy makers are frequently wary of making changes in a field which seems to them to be so replete with emotional conflict. Therefore our focus, on the extended adoption family and the adoption community, aims to bring people together, not only to improve case management, but also to improve the climate in which post-adoption service systems can grow and flourish. We wish to promote a closer working relationship between self-help and professional groups.

A contemporary, universal issue concerns the impact of opening up adoption legislation. Many members of extended adoption families have responded to the increasing visibility of issues such as adoptee and birth parent search, biological identity, and open adoption. Adoptive parents support their adopted child's search for her or his origins; birth parents and adoptees struggle to find a way to relate to each other after contact; adoptive and birth parents struggle to practice open adoption together.

Frequently these new relationships are beautiful and easy, but they are more often difficult. In our experience, too often moves to these new relationships within the extended adoption family are prompted by exposure to new adoption philosophies, which proselytize openness as wonderful and a "right," when the reality can be one of hard struggle, conflict, and frustration.

There is a need therefore for clinical services to help consolidate difficult new relationships, open adoption and post-reunion relationships, and to help the participants deal with the problems that can occur. This area, more than most, requires a great sensitivity in the contemporary adoption scene.

CONCEPTUAL FRAMEWORK

There are four concepts which we have found provide a valuable framework in which to base our clinical work. Each general concept helps to organize management of a particular case, and their combined usage ensures a comprehensive program of assessment and intervention.

The Life Course Development Perspective

The essence of a life course perspective is the understanding that individuals are in a continuous state of flux over their full lifespan. Development does not end with childhood but continues through to old age.

We can borrow from the life course development literature several useful notions:

First, each area of human functioning has a particular trajectory. Some slowly emerge and fade; some grow continuously; some develop early, some late. These trajectories reflect the interaction of constitutional predispositions and environmental circumstances.

Second, transitions between one period of life to another are a constant feature of life course development. The transitions may be from childhood to adolescence to adulthood; from single to married, from marriage to divorce, from wife to widow, from employed to retired. Times of transition are crucial to development in that they represent both threats to stability and opportunities for growth, since old life patterns are shaken and new ones have to be learned. Transitions may or may not be difficult issues, but the ways in which one of the transitions is managed may affect management of later transitions. Many of these transitions are reasonably predictable in terms of timing and sequence, since they reflect generalized social processes.

Third, life course development takes place in both personal time and historical time. Movement through adolescence, for example, was different during the economic depression of the 1930s from movement through adolescence in the 1960s and different again to the 1980s.

Fourth, life span development is strongly affected by capricious life events which have their effects on ability to cope, partly due to the way they interact with transition periods. The loss of a loved one has different effects at different periods of one's life — e.g., if it is "to be expected," is premature, or comes at a time of traumatic changes (e.g., shortly after a divorce). The slings and arrows themselves often come in certain patterns — e.g., road accidents occur more in the young than the old, death of one's parents more when one is middle aged.

The relevance of life course development concepts to post-adoption services is obvious. The *particular* difficulties of adoptee identity become especially acute at times when identity is *generally* a problem (e.g., during the transitions of adolescence or those that follow divorce or death of parents). The *particular* difficulties of adoptee–adoptive parent relations become especially acute at times when family relations are generally a problem (e.g., birth of a new child, children leaving home, children learning to be adults with their parents). The *particular* difficulties of birth parents become especially acute at times when parents find themselves facing difficulties experienced by all parents (e.g., the birth of a new child, realizing one's children have become or are becoming adults).

We have found that in most adoption cases it is necessary to use a life course development framework to guide assessment of each new case. We also find that contemporary problems are frequently linked to events in the past. A purely contemporary focus, such as one might use in much of humanist and behavior therapy, is frequently inadequate. In some cases, this linkage to past events may be best understood in psychodynamic terms, but more often something simpler can be useful. Simply having a birth parent tell the full story of her relinquishment for the first time may be sufficient. The life course development framework reminds us to place contemporary problems in historical time and not solely focus on present issues.

The Social History Perspective

The life course development perspective draws attention to the fact that development takes place in historical as well as personal time. This is particularly pertinent when one deals, as we do here, with the impact of past adoption practice. Adoption placements that took place five years ago are very different from those that took place twenty years ago. Social attitudes have changed and adoption practices have changed. Thirty years ago, the belief that the child should be raised "as if one's own" led to more secrecy and less openness; adoptive parents from five years ago were more likely to have suffered the indignities of having to prove they would be good parents, but are likely to have discussed adoption more openly.

Thirty years ago, a young single woman considering relinquishing her first child was more likely to have been stigmatized and had fewer options and supports available to her, and experienced a childbirth with little or no contact with the child. Five years ago, a young single woman considering relinquishing a child for adoption is more likely to feel that the decision was hers (i.e., free from coercion) because social attitudes, adoption practices, and hospital management are more sensitive to her needs.

Absence of a social history perspective frequently leads to gross misunderstanding. It is very difficult for adoptees today to realize what it was like for their birth mothers when they were teenagers. They often simply translate today's conditions backwards, with the result that they feel more strongly rejected or angry. Adoption workers of today may judge their forebearers overly harshly, failing to recognize that adoption practice, like most of human affairs, is a creature of its times. Adoptees searching for birth parents who turn out to be reluctant to meet them may underestimate the impact of past social stigma and lose opportunities for contact through impatience and lack of insight.

The Traditional Adoption Family

For most of the history of adoption, the primary emphasis has been placement of adoptees with adoptive parents. Once the adoptee entered the adoptive parents' family, the adoptee became "as if born" to them. Psychological ties as well as legal ties to the birth parents were therefore cut to preserve the adoptive family's security. When the adoptee was placed, at birth or close to birth, it was possible to act toward all concerned as if the child was born to the adoptive parents. Adoption in such circumstances is therefore built upon secrecy. Adoptive parents felt, supported by adoption practitioners and the general community, that the child's emotional security and the parent's security was best preserved by submerging any difference from biologically based families. Children therefore grew up not knowing they were adopted, while adoptive parents and often their relatives worked hard to prevent the child from knowing. Of course, the longer the secret was maintained, the harder it was to break, but the greater the likelihood that the secrecy would be broken. A further reason given for wanting to preserve secrecy was the protection of the birth mother. It was argued that single women who gave birth and relinquished would wish to forget that unfortunate period in their lives. The decent thing to do was to pull a veil over these women to allow them to repair their lives and "reputations." This, of course, had the effect of giving adoptive parents the feeling that they could raise their new child without the threat of interference from birth parents turning up unexpectedly, while at the same time giving them the feeling that they were also being socially responsible by helping baby and birth parent out of their trouble.

These are very understandable motivations. Their strength and utility is reflected in the fact that they have underpinned adoption practice for most of this century at least, and continue to be the basis of most contemporary non-relative adoptions despite our use of the past tense to describe them.

Their effects have been, however, to:
- limit awareness of all parties to the adoption process;
- limit awareness of the life course of all parties to the adoption process; and
- limit awareness of the relationships between these parties.

These effects reflect the desire to have the adoptee "disappear" into the adoptive family, to be like any other child.

The major party who disappears from sight is the birth parent. Adoptive parents may have occasionally been told something of the mother, but little else was known to them and usually less to the adoptee. The adoption field itself reflected this. A considerable amount of research and practice focused and still focuses on the teenage pregnancy, pregnancy counseling, and prevention of teenage pregnancy. But once the child is born, the teenage girl turned mother simply drops off the pages of the literature. Only recently has she begun to appear. In addition, as we have already noted, the primary focus in adoption service has been the placement period; we wish to expand this focus to include the full life span.

Raising the child as if born to the adoptive parents requires that the adoptee and adoptive parents be cut off from the birth parents and that the adoptee be cut off from his or her biological origins. The sole relationships that remain are those within the adoptive parents' extended family.

Our concern in this section is with this last point. Although the curtailment of relationships is not primarily based on this argument, it is frequently argued that a child cannot have two sets of parents; in this case, the adoptive parents and the birth parents. Such a situation is felt to be unnatural, confusing, and destructive to the child, as well as confusing and destructive to the parents. It is also felt to be confusing legally.

Yet these arguments are embedded in an ideology which gives primacy to the nuclear family. In many societies, however, children are raised not simply by nuclear families, cut off from other relationships, but by extended families, in which child care is shared by many relatives or by many members of the society. The biological parent is not replaced or threatened by such arrangements, but is strengthened by them. The child also is not confused and conflicted but strengthened by belonging in this rich web of relationships. This is not to say that such arrangements are ideal or have no problems. They emerge from their own particular social conditions and may constitute a burden, but they accomodate the realities of family membership. Our point is that extended families in which there are multiple relationships for child care are not, in fact, unnatural, but are instead quite common. Our unfamiliarity with them tends to have us think that all "parenting" is the same — i.e., if an adoptive parent and a birth parent both have a parental relationship with a child, they will inevitably conflict because they both *want the same thing*. This is a sensible concern, since although one can point to other societies, it is *our* society we are talking about and, rightly or wrongly, that is what has conditioned our notions of parenthood and childhood; but we have failed to accomodate the realities of the child's multiple family membership. Post-adoption clinical services often deal with cases where just such conflicts between adoption and birth parents occur, conflicts that are extremely bitter. Our point, however, is that there are many possible parent–child relationships not typically encountered in nuclear families, which can be successful. As we shall see, post-adoption clinical services frequently deal with quite beautiful joint relationships between adoptive parents, birth parents, and adoptees.

Regardless of what one thinks of what should or could be the relationship between birth parents, adoptive parents, and adoptees, a strong set of relationships continues to exist. The relationships do not require contact or knowledge of each other to develop and continue. Indeed, the very absence of contact and information fuels them. The foundation of these relationships are not contact, information, or exposure, but biological linkages, encrusted with fantasy, fear, hope, anger, and longing. Adoptees fantasize about their birth parents, particularly their birth mother. They wonder what they were like and why they placed them for adoption. These fantasies vary on a continuum; they may be occasional and have little significance for behavior, or they may be constant preoccupations and be of great significance to many areas of functioning. Birth parents, particularly birth mothers, likewise wonder about the child to whom they gave birth. As for adoptees, the extent and significance of this psychological relationship varies considerably; but for a substantial proportion of birth mothers, it is a major part of their lives, a part which is usually a source of pain and anger.

For adoptive parents, the psychological relationship with birth parents tends to fluctuate with the adoptee's concerns about the awareness of his or her biological origins. If the adoptee is drawn into action in this area, so are the adoptive parents. The difference between the adoptive parents and the adopted child's physical appearance can be sufficient to prevent secrecy and important enough to raise questions about biological and cultural origins from the outset. If a child is adopted from another race or country, a psychological relationship exists between the birth culture and the adoptive culture; adoptive parents must consider how they will handle this issue as well as any relationship with the birth parents, who are generally unknown as within traditional adoption families. In the case of adoption of older children, the adoptive parents have to determine how they will relate to the child his or her early childhood history.

The Search For the Missing Members of the Extended Adoption Family

The most publicly significant actions prompted by these psychological relationships are the searches of adoptees and birth parents for each other. Hundreds of thousands of adoptees wish to know more about their origins and actively engage in searches, in order to at least find this information and frequently to make contact with their birth relatives. Hundreds of thousands of birth parents must wish at least to know how their relinquished child has grown up and to explain the circumstances of the relinquishment, and perhaps go on to meet their relinquished child. In many countries, there are considerable legal barriers to such searches; despite this, search, contact, and reunion have grown into major activities in the last 10–15 years.

Not all adoptees or birth parents wish to search; and of those who search, not all wish to meet; of those who meet, not all wish to establish an ongoing relationship. We shall discuss search, contact, and contact outcomes at a later stage; however, the sheer numbers of those searching indicate that regardless of preferred philosophies about encapsulated or non-encapsulated adoptive families, important relationships do exist between adoptive and birth family constellations.

Recognition of these psychological relationships has led several adoption authorities to speak of the adoption triad and of open adoption. The term *adoption triad* emphasized that there are three major parties to the adoption process — the adoptee, the adoptive parents, and the birth parents — all of whom have equal rights and responsibilities, all of whom require attention and services. The term *open adoption* has several meanings. It contrasts with closed adoptive families where the adoptee is raised "as if born to" the adoptive parents; the adoptive parents and birth parents enter into arrangements in which various degress and types of information exchange or contact are maintained, so that the adoptee and birth parents are kept informed about or in touch with each other.

We use the term *extended adoption family* rather than *adoption triad* for several reasons. Adoptees grow older, and many have children of their own. Birth parents grow older, many have more children. Adoptive parents separate, and remarry. The parents of the young single birth mother, who often play such a significant role in the decision to keep or relinquish, grow older and often retain a bond with their first grandchild. The outcome of an adoptee search frequently is not a birth parent (who may have died) but another birth relative.

Our clinical experience is that this web of birth and adoptive relationships is not just between individuals (as implied by the triangle concept) but between family systems and subsystems.

We also wish to remind ourselves of the notion of an extended family when we talk about relationships in adoption. The biologically based extended family exemplified complex interlocking relationships, where an uncle might be like a parent but not a parent, where a cousin might be more like a sibling than an actual brother or sister; where relationships may continue despite a complete absence of contact over many years; where one sub-system may feel ambivalent about members of another sub-system but still share blood relations in common. Relationships which connect adoptive and biological families are in many ways like the relationships in an extended family or extended kinship system.

Finally, by retaining the term *family* we wish to signify that we want to retain the positive qualities of family life and extend them over both the adoptive and birth family systems. We wish to think of both sets of family systems as part of a larger whole. Yet we do not push them together out of some ideological pressure; just as within solely biological extended families, some sections of the family may prefer not to interact very often. Some members of an extended family sub-system may fight with members of another sub-system, may be wary of each other or simply not speak, but they remain related. So it is, we believe, in the extended adoption family.

Like other adoption concepts, our concept of the extended adoption family is a conceptual device that is more or less useful, rather than more or less correct. It is useful in that it prevents a tendency to build adoption practice solely upon the ideal of a nuclear family and so works against the barriers which prevent adoptees from developing a complete sense of identity and prevent birth parents from emerging from limbo. It is also useful in clinical work since it rationalizes a more complete assessment of a client's relationships — relationships built upon both continued contact and fantasy and relationships within family of origin, be it biological or adoptive, and current family. The extended adoption family concept also rationalizes interactions that are *systemic* in nature – interventions that focus on family systems and sub-systems, on *relationships*. An essential principle of such systemic intervention is that action in one part of a system will have consequences in another part of the system; interventions must therefore consider not just the client in isolation, but must either treat the client in relation to others, as in family therapy, or must proceed on the assumption that the system or subsystem itself, not an individual, is "the client" in this situation.

THE ADOPTION COMMUNITY

We have already alluded to our fourth organizing concept: the adoption community. In a large number of post-adoption cases, particularly those involving search, the client is in contact with several community agencies. The searcher may have joined a self-help organization, may have contacted the agencies involved in the original placement, and may be attempting to seek information through several sources and individuals. One of these agencies may have referred the client. Management of the case is frequently improved by integrating resources from these different groups. For example, it is essential that the therapist or counselor know how these agencies work, what their policies are, what they can and cannot do. It is invaluable if the therapist or counselor knows key individuals in these agencies, sometimes in order to ask specific questions, sometimes to act as the client's advocate. Because these agencies and organizations may be in conflict (e.g., self-help organizations may distrust government agencies), it is essential that the therapist or counselor retain sufficient integrity in order to relate to all agencies that might be involved in a case. It is important also to be able to work with *all* members of the extended adoption family. This requires good relationships with all organizations and agencies, many of which may be opposed to each other. For example, birth parent self-help organizations may be lobbying for legislative changes which are being vigorously opposed by adoptive parent organizations. A post-adoption service, however, needs to be in a position where it can take referrals from both organizations and work with both, as a case demands. This may require considerable wisdom and great tact, particularly in cases where the essence of the problem may be conflict between a birth parent and an adoptive parent.

The adoption community concept is relevant not only for work with clients but also for community work. It is tempting to minimize the conflicts that can arise from direct service work by staying clear from anything other than working with clients. But many therapists and counselors can not or do not wish to avoid becoming involved in the social issues surrounding adoption.

The essence of the concept of the adoption community is that all self-help organizations and adoption agencies, no matter what their views, are part of a community of common interest. The adoption community concept is an extension of the extended adoption family concept, from systems of individuals to systems of organizations and services. The term draws attention to the commonalities across these individuals and organizations and to the need for them to work together in a way that emphasizes their connectedness while respecting their differences.

ADOPTION IN HISTORICAL CONTEXT

Our life course and social history concepts inevitably draw attention to the need to place contemporary clinical adoption practice in historical perspective. We shall, for convenience, divide this historical account into two parts: (a) the very long history of adoption that precedes this century; and (b) the history of adoption as it directly impinges on current clients. Our account will inevitably be brief and we urge further reading of what is a fascinating story.

Pre-Modern Adoption

Adoption is an ancient practice, the first known codification of laws, the Hammurabi Code of Babylon, featured extensive codes for the regulation of adoption. Greek, Roman, Chinese, and Indian cultures also used adoption extensively and had complex laws to govern its practice.

The adoptions that took place in these ancient cultures were largely relative adoptions, with the adoptive parent frequently being the adoptee's uncle. It was not unusual for the adoption to take place when the adoptee was a grown child or teenager, a situation in which secrecy about the adoption was not possible. Most adoptees were male. The major motivations for adoption were to do with inheritance and religion. Where there was no child, particularly no male child, to whom property could be passed, adoption was a recognized and acceptable solution. In most of the European–Asian societies which practiced adoption, religious worship was closely tied up with ancestry and clan. To preserve spiritual continuity, the family needed to continue, and adoption was needed to preserve this continuity. Adoption was also used to cement ties between families to ensure political stability.

Adoption is, and was, little known in Africa. It has been argued that this is a function of several factors: the relative absence of ancestor worship, the relative absence of accumulated property among hunters and gatherers, and, most importantly, the prevalence of polygamy or extended kinship systems rather than nuclear families. Where the social norm is that children are raised by the group rather than the immediate nuclear family, discontinuities in the biological family caused by death or infertility can be handled without the need for special laws or procedures. Formal adoption, for similar reasons, is, and has been, relatively unknown in the Pacific Islands and Australian aboriginal culture.

Adoption in the Twentieth Century

British, American, and Australian adoption laws were first introduced in the period from 1890s to the 1920s. The major rationale for these laws was to recognize adoption as a legitimate social practice and to regulate it in order to prevent what were seen as excesses and ambiguities.

Children in poor houses or those who roamed the streets were frequently forced into child labor. Adults could avoid paying appropriate wages by considering such children as adoptees, while at the same time feeling worthy citizens by rescuing such children from a disadvantaged life. In the United States, the famous Orphan Train took children from the industrial cities to start a new life in the country. In Australia, aboriginal children were removed from their families in the name of their salvation, in order to be trained as house servants.

A review of Hansard, the parliamentary record of debate in Australian Parliaments, is instructive for the attitudes it reveals. As in the United States, Australian adoption laws are state rather than federal laws. The debates reveal several themes which generally appeared in the order listed: a desire to protect the interests of adoptive parents, a desire to protect the good name of the birth mother, and, finally, a desire to protect the interests of the child.

This shift, from an adult focus to a child focus, is typical of most Western adoption laws. The now generally agreed-upon child welfare focus of adoption law, which gives precedence to what is believed to be the child's best interests, is a relatively recent phenomenon. For most of this century, and therefore for most of the placements that shaped the lives of today's older clients, adoption law and practice was slanted toward the perceived interests of adoptive parents and the perceived interests of the birth mother, with the emphasis on the family. There were several widely held attitudes that shaped adoption law and practice. Attitudes toward sexuality were such that the young single woman who became pregnant was the subject of often severe rejection by family and society. Abortion was difficult, if not impossible, and relinquishment was seen as an act of redemption. Charity to the poor and disadvantaged was a central middle-class value, as was the belief that white middle-class values were the essence of goodness. Taking a child from poverty and disadvantage and raising her or him in proper society was seen as an act of virtue. Such were the values of the respectable middle class; however, there was always a fear that poor breeding would always win out, that the adopted child might turn out to be "no good" — a fear which could easily turn to rejection if life became difficult.

For most of this century, birth mothers had little choice but to relinquish a child born "out of wedlock." There was no effective form of contraception; male sexual attitudes were exploitative of women, particularly women of a "lower" social or racial class; abortion was not generally available; and social services to enable single mothers to parent their child were absent or primitive. Keeping a child was regarded as selfish, inconsiderate, and further evidence of moral turpitude.

Institutions for the single mother were commonplace. Frequently, these institutions were harsh and moralistic with a strong if not complete emphasis on relinquishment. Institutional care was commonplace for babies and young children who were relinquished, orphaned, or without their families for other reasons. These institutions also were often harsh, moralistic, and under-financed.

There were more children than prospective adoptive parents. Prospective adoptive parents were able to pick and choose with relatively little vetting of suitability on the parent's side. This picture has gradually changed over the last twenty years to the current situation, where prospective adoptive parents outnumber children available for adoption and prospective parents are now assessed to insure their suitability. The massive shift in the prospective adoptive parent–prospective adoptee ratio that has taken place in the last twenty years is largely due to the substantial drop in the number of children being relinquished for adoption. Currently, less than 10% of young single pregnant women opt to place their children for adoption; this figure is quite consistent across North America, Europe, and Australia. Some who work with pregnant teenagers, particularly in the United States, where rates of teenage pregnancy are particularly high, have begun to call for a renewed emphasis on the adoption option, arguing that keeping the child is too costly for all concerned, including the taxpayer.

Partly in response to the unavailability of locally born children, adoption of children born in other countries has become commonplace. Intercountry adoptions have been seen not only as a response to infertility, but also as a humanitarian endeavour in which children from Third World countries can be rescued from disadvantage. Paradoxically, at the same time, local interracial adoption has been attacked as a form of cultural imperialism by racial minority groups. Some countries, expressing similar concerns, have forbidden international adoptions or have attempted to curtail them.

In the last fifteen years, children who previously were considered not suitable for adoption have been adopted in increasing numbers. Older children who languished in institutions are being adopted, as are handicapped children. Adoption is seen as an integral part of the deinstitutionalization movement and as an important component of permanency planning for children in care.

These shifts in placement practice have been accompanied by a general shift from closed attitudes to more open attitudes. Adoption is more openly discussed in adoptive families who adopted in the last fifteen years than it was in the period before. There is a greater recognition that the adoptive family can remain secure and living, while permitting the adoptee to find his own way to his origins. Kirk (1984) articulated these different adoption styles and contributed to the shift to greater openness. Sorosky, Baran, and Pannor (1978) also contributed to this movement by emphasizing the inherent relationships of the adoption triangle — adoptee, adoptive parents, and birth parents. Triseliotis (1973) contributed through his classic study of adoptees' search for their origins. Gradually, the adoption community has come to accept that open discussion and acknowledgement of relations across the extended adoption family is in the best interests of the child (frequently by this stage an adult).

There have been several moves to establish adoption placements which are, to various degrees, open from the outset. Birth parents may help choose the adoptive parents for their child, may arrange to communicate with the adoptive parents on an ongoing basis, or may arrange to interact directly with the adoptive parents as the child grows up. While these arrangements are controversial, it is not unusual for the birth parents to play a role in the choice of the adoptive parents for their child.

In most countries and regions, adoption has come to be a matter for government agencies and private welfare organizations (both religious and child welfare). However, for many years, there have been private adoption services run mostly by lawyers, by obstetricians, and sometimes by persons with business interests. These services arrange adoptions for a fee and have as their clients both birth and adoptive parents. The practices of some of these private practitioners have been subject to criticism. While less common in Australia, they are still very active in the United States, particularly in California, where almost 80% of contemporary adoption placements are carried out by private practitioners.

Changes in the adoption community this century have been immense. Adoption placement rates have dropped rapidly from high levels, social attitudes have shifted from punitiveness to greater acceptance, and adoption has become more openly discussed. These shifts have been substantial and rapid. In some places, of course, the older attitudes and practices can still be found, and in others clear vestiges can still be seen. But change has taken place, and it has taken place within the lifetime of most of those who are now adoptees, birth parents, and adoptive parents. There does remain an aftermath from past attitudes and practices which continues to affect, very deeply, the adult lives of those touched by adoption. It is this aftermath which forms the nub of clinical practice in post-adoption services.

THE CONTRIBUTION OF LITERATURE AND RESEARCH

There are a number of studies and accounts of personal experience which have contributed to the recognition of adoption as a life course experience. The following are representative but by no means inclusive:

In 1953 Jean M. Paton conducted what was probably the earliest research on adopted adults, finding that adoptees have a need for information with respect to their biological origins. Paton also concluded that adoptees of any age are considered children and never become true adults in society's eyes. Hers was the earliest call for legislative reform and the need for contact registers. Her 1954 book, *Adoptees Break Silence*, provided an important early impetus for reform.

David Kirk's 1964 work, *Shared Fate: A Theory of Adoption and Mental Health*, was a significant early contribution to our understanding that adoptive parents face unique parenting tasks. By acknowledging to themselves and their adopted children that adoptive parenthood is different and involves loss, they are able to form a bond with their adopted child, who also experiences the loss of separation from birth parents — thus affirming a shared fate.

Alexina McWinnie's 1966 study, *Adopted Children and How They Grow Up*, another early investigation of adoptees, concluded that it is not in the best interests of the adoptee to be precluded from having access to factual information about birth parents.

John Triseliotis in his 1973 study, *In Search of Origins: The Experience of Adopted Persons*, was the first researcher to explore the sociological and psychological effects of allowing adoptees free access to their origins upon reaching the age of majority. His research was a major contribution to the law change in England, which granted adult adoptees access to their original birth certificates.

Florence Fisher's *The Search for Anna Fisher* (1973) provided impetus for the adoptee self-help and legislative reform movement in the United States. The founder of the Adoptee Liberty Movement Association (ALMA), Fisher inspired thousands of adoptees in the United States to undertake a search for their birth parents.

Betty Jean Lifton's *Twice Born: Memoirs of an Adopted Daughter* (1975) and her 1979 book, *Lost and Found: The Adoption Experience* are both compelling evocations of the adoption experience, and make a powerful argument for the essential right of all adoptees to have access to their birthright — open records and the opportunity for reunion with birth parents.

Sorosky, Baran, and Pannor's 1976 book, *The Adoption Triangle: the Effects of the Sealed Record on Adoptees, Birth Parents, and Adoptive Parents*, provides a comprehensive view, based on extensive interviews, of the long-term effects of the adoption experience on triad members. The authors also presented an extensive critique of outmoded adoption practices with recommendations for change.

Mary Kathleen Benet's *The Politics of Adoption* (1976) is an important analysis of the moral and political issues at the heart of the adoption experience and adoption practice. Robert J. Lifton's foreword to this volume is a compelling statement of the need for openness in adoption.

Joseph H. Davis, in his 1979 article, "The Pediatric Role in Adoption," became an early advocate of open records, and called on physicians to respond to the needs of the adoption triad.

Robin Winkler and Margaret van Keppel's 1984 study *Relinquishing Mothers in Adoption: Their Long Term Adjustment* is the first carefully controlled study of the long term effects of relinquishing a child on the current adjustment of mothers. This study confirmed and documented in detail that relinquishment has a profound and continuing negative effect on the emotional well-being of the mothers. Winkler and van Keppel urge the establishment of official contact registers, the provision of support and counseling facilities for birth mothers, and changes in legislation to allow adoptees access to their original birth certificates.

David Brodzinsky's work, published in 1984, on new perspectives on adoption revelation is an important contribution to our knowledge of how and at what age adoptees come to understand the meaning of adoption in their lives.

Sue Midford's work in Australia in 1986, concerned with developing a model and measure of adoptee identity, is especially noteworthy because it gives us, for the first time, a multi-factorial psychometric measure of adoptee identity.

THE CURRENT SCENE

Most contemporary adoptions are initiated by a child's own blood relatives. The number of contemporary adoptions remains small compared to 25 years ago, but is nevertheless a continuing and important part of child welfare practice.

It has been generally agreed that the guiding principle behind all adoption placements should be the best interests of the child. This is accompanied by a second policy goal — permanency planning: the desire to have children in as long term and stable a caring relationship as can be arranged.

The indignities and dangers of multiple caretakers and of institutionalizated care are to be avoided whenever possible — hence the desire to find adopters for children who would previously have had to languish in such arrangements.

The contemporary field of adoption is a field of secondary importance in the current welfare scene. It has been overtaken by more urgent and widespread issues such as child abuse, teenage pregnancy, and homeless youth. There have been some who felt it was a middle-class endeavor, rather than one which responded primarily to the needs of the disadvantaged, since children were generally taken from disadvantage into a more affluent class of adoptive parents. This judgment plays down the fact that adoption frequently represented the only way out for very young disadvantaged children.

Our concern in this book is to correct this perception of adoption as a dying field. Adoption services have a huge backlog of cases which they have only begun to recognize and acknowledge. The very compassion which drove adoption for most of this century needs to be redirected toward post-adoption services. It may not be the same agencies that will take up the task — many of the older agencies may be unable to shift orientation. New services with new staff who are nevertheless aware of old practices and attitudes may be needed to underwrite the newer post-adoption services.

We have organized our book very simply. Chapter 2 deals with the organization of post-adoption services; chapter 3 discusses the basic issues in the clinical practice of adoption. The next three chapters deal with each member, in turn, of the adoption family: the birth parents, the adoptive parents, and the adoptee. Each chapter places that person in a life course perspective relative to adoption. The major presenting problems are reviewed in developmental sequence, followed by accounts of how they are handled in clinical practice.

Our penultimate chapter will discuss the growing demands of the newer developments in the adoption field, including the adoption of children with special needs, the adoption of children from overseas, and the clinical implications for the persons affected by the new reproductive technologies.

We bring our book to a close by a consideration of the tasks for the future in relation to the provision of post-adoption services.

Chapter 2
Delivery of Post-Adoption Services

Within the adoption community, the need for post-adoption services has been widely recognized, and many diverse programs have been developed. As we have developed a broader and deeper understanding of the impact of adoption on people's lives, we have come to see that many models of service delivery are possible and, indeed, appropriate. At this stage in the development of post-adoption services, the demand appears to be exceeding the resources available; this pattern is likely to continue for some time, as people feel more and more able to "go public" about their adoption experience.

Adoption is a fact of people's lives, and presents them with different challenges depending on their developmental tasks, life events, and resources at any one time. Adoption does not necessarily imply pathology. The need for services is both normal and healthy. Whether services are remedial or preventative, all requests for services should be dealt with sensitively and creatively. The level of importance of the fact of the adoption is idiosyncratic to each each individual client, and should not be minimized or exaggerated according to the biases of the service provider.

The full range of post-adoption services must be able to respond to all of the following needs.

For the extended adoption family

- background and/or ongoing information pertaining directly to persons affected by an adoption experience;
- information and education about current adoption issues, laws, and practices;
- assistance and support from peers, in specific areas (e.g., adoptive parenting, searching);

- counseling and therapy for individuals, couples, and families affected by adoption;
- crisis intervention;
- group therapy; and
- advocacy.

For the adoption community

- community education;
- consultation;
- training;
- lobbying and law reform;
- evaluation and research; and
- networking of resources.

Post-adoption services must be available to all persons who require them, regardless of their status in the extended adoption family; how, when, or where their adoption experience occurred; their financial means; or their current legal and geographic status (National Model Statement, Children's Home Society of Minnesota, 1984).

For a variety of reasons, many people will not return to the agency with which they were originally affiliated. For example, some adoptive parents believe that they have failed to meet the placement agency's expectations if they return in later years with difficulties; on the other hand, many birth parents feel that they were poorly treated by the agency that placed their child and do not wish to return for any assistance, other than to lodge a complaint or seek information. People need to obtain services from sources other than those connected with their original adoption experience.

We believe that it is neither practical nor appropriate for any one organization, agency, or individual to attempt to provide *all* necessary post-adoption services. It is the integration and availability of a wide range of services which will provide for the diverse needs outlined above. While the range is limitless, the format of services can be described in three major categories: self-help, professional help, and integrated services. We believe that all of these services are essential and should be complementary. Many programs, indeed, incorporate two or three types of services.

SELF-HELP GROUPS

The term "self-help" applies only to those services which are organized, facilitated, and provided by those personally affected by an adoption experience for the benefit of themselves and their peers. Such people usually organize themselves into groups, and the group becomes the basis for the service delivery. Self-help groups are usually autonomous of agency involvement. There are many different types of self-help groups in the post-adoption area, serving all members of the adoption triad. These groups may be oriented toward providing peer support, working toward legislative and practice change, sharing knowledge, skills and resources (e.g., search groups), or all three. Some groups focus on the needs and interests of only one member of the triad, while others cater to all members.

In accordance with the "self-help" ideology and tradition, adoption self-help groups are typically financially independent and self-supporting: their funds are drawn from membership fees and fees charged for specific services (e.g., workshops, publications, and search assistance). The leaders and facilitators are usually democratically elected, and the operations of the group are regulated by pre-defined procedures or bylaws.

Self-help groups provide post-adoption services in a limitless number of ways, both formally and informally. Membership of a self-help group is often a powerful means of reducing isolation and alienation on the basis of shared experiences. Members share advice, information, and skills, both formally and informally. Telephone "counseling" and assistance is available when required, and emotional support is freely available to those experiencing difficulties; more specifically, search-oriented groups legitimize both the "right to know" and the search.

Examples of the various post-adoption self-help groups are as follows:

Birth Parent Groups

Birth parent groups vary in composition and focus. Membership may be limited to birth mothers only, to both birth mothers and birth fathers, or primarily to birth parents but with other members of the triad and the adoption community welcomed, either as full members or associate members. The focus of any birth parent support group may be any one or combination of the following:
- support (there is much emphasis on the sharing of personal stories and experiences through informal links, meetings, and newsletters);
- community education and attitude change, especially to raise the profile and status of birth parents (through letters and submission writing, public speaking, and discussion groups);
- lobbying for legislative and practice reform;
- search support and assistance. (Increasingly, birth parents are concerned with seeking a reunion with the adoptee, and the self-help group provides them not only with the practical assistance and emotional support they require, but also legitimizes their search and assists them in integrating the past with the present — typically a very difficult task for birth parents).

The therapeutic value of birth parent self-help groups will be discussed in more detail in chapter 4.

Adoptive Parent Groups

Adoptive parent groups also vary in composition and focus. The most common type of groups are for the adoptive parents of children with special needs (emotional difficulties or developmental disabilities) and transracially adopted children (in-country or inter-country). Self-help groups for adoptive parents of children adopted by traditional means have been typically slow to develop. For a long time, the assumption was widely promoted that adoptive parenting was not different from other forms of parenting, and it was thought to be counterproductive to emphasize any difference. In more recent years, however, we have seen the development of adoptive parent self-help groups that have attempted to respond to a specific issue, such as the opening of adoption records, adolescent crises, and the search movement. The focus of the adoptive parent groups are:
- emotional and social support for adoptive parents and their children (meetings, informal contact, family activities, newsletters);
- community education (public speaking, seminars and conferences);
- lobbying around practice and legislative matters.

The therapeutic value of adoptive parent self-help groups will be discussed further in chapter 5.

Adoptee Groups

Self-help groups for adoptees are typically for adult adoptees who are concerned with issues of search and reunion. In so doing, they are also concerned with:
- providing emotional and social support (informal contact, meetings, newsletters);
- search assistance and intermediary services (if desired);
- community education (public speaking, publications, seminars, conferences);
- advocacy on behalf of members; and
- lobbying for legislative and practice reform.

Many adoptee self-help groups have extended their membership to include other members of the adoption triad and the extended adoption family. Some of these groups have nonetheless remained more adoptee-focused, while others have become more involved in issues that would concern all members.

Chapter 6 will describe in more detail the therapeutic value of adoptee self-help groups.

Adoption triad groups.

Self-help groups open to all members of the adoption triad enable members to better understand the whole spectrum of feelings and attitudes common to

the adoption experience (Floud, 1982). Commonly held stereotypes and myths are quickly dispelled as the different members of the adoption triad begin to know and accept each other as fellow human beings who have essentially suffered similar experiences of loss, shame, guilt, alienation and confusion. As a result, many of the conflicts and tensions inherent in the adoption experience are overcome, and members work cooperatively toward:
- support, information and resource sharing;
- community education and attitude change; and
- legislative and practice reform.

While adoption triad self-help groups are both healing and constructive for personal group members and the adoption community in general, groups that cater only to the interests of one member of the triad are also necessary. Such groups tend to be more powerful in their validation of the common experiences of being an adoptee, birth parent, or an adoptive parent. They reduce the felt isolation and alienation, and contribute to the rapid restoration of self-esteem and self-confidence. Both triad groups *and* limited membership groups should be available. They will meet different persons' needs at different times.

However, in the area of legislative and practice reform, triad groups have generally had more credibility, both in the adoption community and the wider community. They are seen to present a unified voice. For too long the conflicts of interest among and between the triad groups has impeded the adoption reform movement.

A significant proportion of members of the extended adoption family will only seek and receive post-adoption services from within the self-help sector, others will only seek services from the professional sector, while others will utilize a combination of both types of services.

PROFESSIONAL SERVICES

Professional post adoption services differ along various dimensions — public–private, agency–individual, specialist–generic, limited–unlimited, and "non profit"–"for profit." Examples of the range of post adoption services include:

— Adoption placement agencies which limit the availability of services to past clients, and only as required (e.g., counseling and the provision of background or updated information).

— Adoption placement agencies which have a post-adoption service available to anyone regardless of previous affiliations. Such agencies may have workers who only do post-adoption work, or it may be the responsibility of all the placement workers. In addition to providing services as requested, these agencies often offer educational workshops and therapeutic support groups.

— Adoption placement agencies which promote adoption as a lifelong process and incorporate a full range of educative, support, and therapeutic services in their total service program. These agencies often incorporate post-adoption awareness into their pre-adoptive counseling program, through discussion groups, information sessions and by encouraging early membership in self-help groups. While most such service programs appear to cater especially to adoptive parents, an increasing number are also becoming oriented toward meeting the needs of the birth parents in a similar manner.

— Adoption-oriented agencies which do not arrange adoptions. Some such agencies were previously placement agencies, but have since altered their service programs. However, they continue to provide post-adoption services to past clients. Others provide services to clients regardless of their previous affiliations. The full range of post-adoption programs are typically available from agencies of this nature.

— Child welfare-oriented agencies, part of whose mandate is to provide a range of services around adoption, including post-adoption counseling.

— Mental health organizations and individuals (private practitioners) who provide a wide range of treatment oriented services to children, adults, and families. Some of these organizations may also provide in-patient or residential treatment. The degree of post-adoption expertise varies according to the experience and training of personnel.

— Finally, private individuals or organizations that provide a very specific service — for example, search consultants.

A recent trend has been to train both adoption (placement) specialists and more generically oriented professionals in post-adoption matters, in order to increase the knowledge and skill base in the community. This will help in meeting the increasing demand for post-adoption services. A number of manuals and training packages have recently been prepared (Bourguignon and Watson, 1987, a,b,; Grabe, 1986).

The financing of professional post-adoption services has proven to be both complex and controversial. The dilemma for many service providers has been whether or not post-adoption services should be provided free of charge to the recipient or subsidized. This dilemma is more apparent in Australia and the United Kingdom, where agencies providing post-adoption services are typically financed wholly or partially through state funds, agency funds, or charitable and benevolent trusts. A number of private agencies and private practitioners are contracted to provide services by another organization (usually the state), either because this is more economical or because specific specialized skills are required.

On the whole, professional post-adoption services are purchased by the recipients as follows:

- free of charge (fully subsidized);
- fee-for-service, not adjusted according to financial means;
- fee-for-service, adjusted according to financial means; and
- third party payments (e.g., health insurance, subsidies available to the adoptive parents of children with special needs).

Many professional post-adoption service agencies incorporate triad members or the self-help groups in their service programs, or actively refer clients to self-help groups. The integration of self-help and professional services can occur in many different ways, some of which will now be discussed.

INTEGRATED SERVICES

It is our belief that a close partnership can exist between the professional and the self-help sectors; however, we assert that there is no model for how this can best happen. The nature of the partnership will depend on the overall availability of services in any one area; historical, legal, and geographical considerations; and the needs and personalities involved. Examples of integrated services are as follows:

First, there are post-adoption centers where salaried and trained volunteer staff (who are all members of the adoption triad) provide programs of information, education, and counseling to all members of the adoption community (Brown, 1983). Such organizations forge a strong link between the members of the adoption triad and the professional sector (adoption and non-adoption). The sectors usually appear to be more credible to each other and there is a greater readiness for dialogue and learning. They are especially important for persons who require professional services but are mistrustful, because of past experiences, of consulting with professionals. There need be no limit to the type of services available from such centers; the program of services depends on the resources available, the creativity of the staff, and the identified needs.

Additionally, many professional post-adoption services include members of the adoption triad in their programs. This can be done in many different ways:
- triad members who feel comfortable talking about their experiences meet with others individually or in groups with others who are beginning to reflect on their individual and collective adoption experience;
- triad members may assist in the facilitation of support groups;
- triad members often volunteer their services to agencies to assist with community education programs and various administrative tasks; and
- triad members are asked to talk of their personal experiences to prospective adoptive parents, so as to heighten their awareness of the lifelong process of adoption. Personal experiences can address and challenge persistent stereotypes and myths surrounding adoption.

Delivery of Post-Adoption Services

Some state departments of adoption have contributed funds and resources to various self-help groups, an acknowledgement of their contribution to post-adoption services, to assist in their work. Such action may consolidate the working partnership that exists, but it may also threaten the autonomy of the self-help group. This is an issue to be considered by self-help groups.

Finally, an increasingly popular partnership between the self-help and professional sectors is the formation of regional and national coordinating committees. These draw membership from all professional and self-help organizations involved in adoption and post-adoption. Such committees address areas of interest to all membership groups, negotiate around areas of conflict, facilitate the networking of resources, challenge the barriers to communication between sectors, engage in community education through joint conferences and media coverage, and lobby for adoption reform. In addition to the working relationships that ensue through such organizations, the committees provide an important forum for service providers to become involved in policy and other lay matters, which are equally as important as clinical issues in the area of post-adoption services.

Chapter 3

Basic Clinical Issues

This chapter will describe those issues that are fundamental to the provision of all therapeutic post-adoption services. Much of what is to be said will echo the concerns of those members of the adoption triad who have sought professional services themselves.

The members of the extended adoption family will seek therapeutic services for as many reasons as there will be requests for services. They may have identified their presenting problem as being directly related to their adoption experience, or they may seek assistance for other matters with the issue of adoption being raised at some stage of the contact, be it intake, assessment, therapy and counseling, or closure. Regardless of the manner in which the issue of adoption is presented to the practitioner, it is imperative that the practitioner know the impact that adoption can have on people's lives, and also, how best to respond to the issue from a therapeutic perspective.

PREPARING OURSELVES TO WORK WITH THE EXTENDED ADOPTION FAMILY

Before we can begin to understand the personal situations of the people who will seek our services, we need to understand about adoption generally. A frequent dilemma for the therapist is determining to what extent a person's presenting problems are adoption related. There is no formula for solving this dilemma; the answer is likely to evolve as the client and therapist work together. The therapist who is more informed about adoption will be more responsive to his or her client, and will not run the risk of minimizing the impact of the adoption experience.

Too often, adoptees, birth parents, and adoptive parents who have sought assistance feel rejected and discounted because their adoption experience was not considered to be a significant factor in their lives. Alternatively, many have felt that there has been too much focus on adoption to the exclusion of other important events and people in their lives.

FUNDAMENTAL CONCEPTS

The two fundamental concepts which must be understood by the post-adoption practitioner are: (a) that the impact of the adoption can have a profound effect on the lives of members of the extended adoption family; and (b) that adoption is a risk factor in people's lives, and will have a different impact at different life stages, depending on the person's understanding and meaning of the adoption experience; his or her emotional and social resources; and other life circumstances at any time.

Common Issues

Some common issues, experienced by each of the members of the adoption triad, are:

1. loss and trauma
2. guilt, shame, and inadequacy
3. disturbing influences on self-image, identity
4. loss of power in directing the course of one's life
5. rejection, and the continuing fear of further rejection
6. isolation and alienation
7. lowered self-esteem
8. unresolved grief

GUIDELINES

The following guidelines will assist the beginning post-adoption practitioner in developing more effective therapeutic relationships with members of the extended adoption family.

1. The clinician will need to understand the adoption practices, values, and assumptions which were prevalent at the time the person's original adoption experience took place. The therapist may need to encourage the person to understand the experiences of other members of the triad and of the extended adoption family.
2. Understanding the subtleties of the adoption experience will greatly assist the therapist in establishing rapport with the client.

3. A knowledge of developmental life stages and tasks will enhance the therapist's understanding of the specific adoption issues with which the client is struggling.
4. Be aware that members of the adoption triad are more likely to be reluctant to seek professional services, due to earlier negative experiences; as a consequence, they are likely to be sensitive to perceived judgment.
5. The adoption triad member's need for privacy and time is often more marked. For many, the adoption experience will have been shrouded in secrecy; they will need to "come out" in their own time, and it is important that they exercise control, perhaps for the first time, in this important area of their life.
6. Be aware that a person's feelings about adoption can be intense and painful; a characteristic response as they begin to explore feelings is "approach–avoidance." Acknowledging the intensity of feeling and the pain is more constructive than simply focusing on the ambivalence.
7. Be sure to create an environment in which the expression of intense feeling is possible; in particular, anger, rage, and sadness about the powerlessness the client has experienced in relation to major life events (e.g., family creation, separation from family members). Additional therapeutic guidelines, specific to birth parents, adoptees, and adoptive parents will be discussed in chapters 4, 5, and 6 respectively.

Guidelines for Self-Assessment

Regardless of the nature of their work, it is essential that therapists engage in self-assessment of their values and assumptions regarding the particular issues the client presents. This is especially important in working with adoption-related issues. The topic and events of adoption typically evoke powerful reactions from all involved.

Many people who have been personally affected by an adoption experience also work in the field. While this background certainly sensitizes a therapist to many of the issues, he or she must also be aware of his or her own biases and issues, in order to avoid the creation of unnecessary difficulties for those with whom he or she is working. The therapist must feel comfortable and able to work with issues of loss, separation, attachment, anger, control, and trust. They must be careful to work at the client's pace and avoid a tendency to urge her or him on (e.g., in regard to searching); The therapist who is also a member of a triad must refrain from using his or her experience as the only frame of reference.

We believe that the first step in the process of self-assessment is reflecting on one's personal experiences, attitudes, and values regarding the issues central to the adoption experience. Many non-adoption life events can result

Basic Clinical Issues   33

in similar patterns of adjustment and dysfunction. The following checklist will assist in the self-assessment process.

How did you first learn about adoption, from whom, and how were the first impressions modified by subsequent experiences?

What are your reactions to and feelings about the labels and stereotypes so often used by the community and the media, such as: "orphan," "bastard," "illegitimate," "bad seed," "unwed mother," "given up," "they never turn out well" (reference to adoptees) and "damaged goods?"

What are your reactions to practices which are becoming increasingly common in adoption today — adoptees and birth parents searching for one another, openness in adoption, adoption of older children?

What has been your experience with separation and loss, either marital or otherwise?

Have you ever experienced the abrupt termination or interruption of a relationship for which you were unprepared, and which resulted in a sense of confusion and lack of resolve (e.g., as a child or as a result of divorce)?

Have you ever experienced an unexpected or premature loss and bereavement, such as miscarriage or the premature death of a child? Such losses are analogous to the pre-adoptive experiences of adoptive parents and the adoptee–birth parent losses experienced in the relinquishment process.

Have you an interest in or experience with family reunions (immediate family members and distant relatives) and genealogical history (experiences which are, to some extent, analogous to search and reunion experiences)?

What is your experience with health problems in which an accurate diagnosis was dependent on genetic information or your family's medical history? (Many adoptees face great difficulties because they do not have access to medical genetic background information, because of the "sealed records" phenomenon).

Many adoption self-help groups will welcome membership and participation from the therapeutic community. Such participation is helpful both for the beginning post-adoption practitioner and for the experienced professional, because the experience of listening to members of the adoption triad talk freely provides insights that are otherwise not easily obtained.

Client Assessment

Obtaining relevant and detailed information about the client is a necessary part of all good clinical practice. This is especially the case in post-adoption services. Most standard procedures apply. In addition, the therapist's personal style and particular therapeutic approach will determine the manner in which information about the client is sought. It is the nature and detail of this information which will determine the quality of the therapist's intervention.

Understanding the information from a developmental perspective will also be advantageous.

The first opportunity to obtain information is likely to be at the time of "intake." For those practitioners who utilize an intake system, asking some questions about the adoption experience at that time will assist the therapist in preparation for the first interview. Given the high proportion of people in the community who have had an adoption experience, we suggest that practitioners in generic agencies or practices ask all of their prospective clients, at intake, whether or not they have had an adoption experience.

The intake interview (typically via the telephone) usually seeks from the client relevant personal details (name, age, marital status, family membership, occupation, address, and contact telephone number) and a description of current difficulties.

To prepare both the therapist and the client for dealing with adoption-related issues, we also suggest obtaining the following additional information:

1. brief description of their adoption experience (what, where, when and who it involved);
2. the degree to which the client thinks his/her current difficulties are adoption-related;
3. a brief history of the difficulties;
4. other practitioners whom they have previously consulted with concerning these difficulties;
5. whether they are or have been a member of any adoption self-help or support group.

Be especially careful with the issues of confidentiality and privacy. Prospective clients may not have told significant family members about their adoption experience. They may experience difficulty during intake and while making appointments because they have not shared their experience with others.

Following intake, the more formal assessment phase commences. Because of the volume and nature of the information being sought, the practitioner is likely to require at least two sessions before moving into the intervention phase. There are several areas of inquiry that constitute assessment. Each will be discussed separately.

In addition to obtaining information about the client's presenting problems, the following suggestions will elicit information relevant to working with the adoption issues.

Basic Clinical Issues

Have the client tell his or her adoption story. Encourage her or him to provide as much detail as possible; ask questions that will fill in the gaps as the story evolves; encourage him or her to express their feelings as he or she tells the story, and allow as much time as is necessary to recount and clarify the significant events. "Telling the story" can be a very powerful experience for both the client and the therapist. It may begin slowly, especially if rapport is still somewhat tentative, and may take a number of sessions to complete. If the client's knowledge of his or her story is incomplete because he or she was not told (not uncommon for adoptees) or because he or she has forgotten (not uncommon for birth parents), it is useful for the client to go away and seek the missing information from hospital or adoption agency records. It is important to seek information not only about the actual adoption placement, but also about subsequent events relevant to the adoption experience.

Identify those areas that have been subject to denial and/or shrouded in secrecy.

What meaning does the client ascribe to the adoption experience? How does he or she think it has affected the course of their life, negatively and positively?

Elicit details about other significant life-events (positive and negative). How did these events impact on the adoption experience, or vice versa?

Obtain information about the client's family system. Be sure to include the family of origin and the current family. How has the adoption experience impacted on the family system? (The use of graphic procedures to represent the family system will be discussed later in this section, under Specific Techniques.)

Obtain additional information. Ask about other professionals consulted, the outcome of these consultations, and other attempts the client has made to deal with his or her current difficulties, including self-help and support group experiences.

Assessment of the Current Situation

In addition to making an assessment of the client's functioning in all areas (physical, cognitive, emotional and social) it is important to elicit the following information about the client.

Current level of stress. What else are they having to deal with at this time, are there any connections with the adoption experience?

Coping Styles. Are these effective; how have they been affected by the adoption experience?

Current support, from family, friends, and the community. Is the available support conditional upon the continuing denial or suppression of the adoption experience? Does the client receive support specifically in relation to the adoption experience? How do family and friends feel about his or her adoption experience?

Knowledge of members of his or her adoption triad. What were their experiences around the time of the adoption, and how do they feel now? Do they have some understanding of his or her likely experiences?

Use of Developmental Information and Normative Data

A developmental perspective and a sound knowledge of normative data will greatly assist the therapist in understanding the outcome of the interaction between their client's adoption-related experiences and cognitive, emotional, and social development. It is often the case that various development tasks (e.g., attachment, identity formation, dependence–independence) are significantly disrupted by an adoption-related experience. For example, the disruption of children's attachments during the first years of life; lack of information about one's background can detrimentally effect the process of developing a sound sense of self; and a pregnancy during adolescence has serious consequences for the mother's sense of belonging to her family and for her developing self-image as a woman.

Developmental psychologists, in particular Erikson and Piaget, have provided comprehensive empirical information about the stages of normal development. Bourguignon and Watson (1987a) provide a useful summary of relevant developmental and normative data, based on the work of Erikson, Piaget, and Kohlberg.

Use of Psychometric Tests

To our knowledge, only one psychometric measure has been developed for use with an adopted population. Midford (1986) has developed a multifactorial psychometric measure of adoptee identity. The measure consists of 25 items, which comprise two scales, the Biological Identity Scale, and the Curiosity Scale. The Biological Identity Scale measures the adoptee's concern with his or her biologic–genetic knowledge of self and sense of belonging in biological time. The Curiosity Scale measures the adoptee's interest in obtaining information about biological origins and birth family.

The use of psychometric tests, standardized for use with the general population, is at the discretion of each therapist, and will depend on familarity with particular tests and on the questions to which he or she are seeking answers.

Bourguignon and Watson (1987a) express caution in the use of psychometric tests with adopted children. They state that it is important to recognize two facts:

> First, many psychological tests compare the child being tested with normal, non-traumatized children. Second, these same tests frequently suggest a potential for "higher" functioning. Such tests should be based on current functioning, not potential functioning, and any conclusions drawn must be carefully and critically analyzed in the context of the child's background and experience (p.17).

Use of Graphic Representations

The use of graphic techniques to depict family history and family relationships in adoption has been described by Grabe (1986) and Hartman (1979, 1984). Grabe (1986) describes a technique devised by Anderson called the *Famograph*. The Famograph is a technique that helps children understand what has happened in their lives and place it in historical context. It assists the child in integrating his/her past with the present. It is especially useful for children who have experienced life with a number of families. It helps the child remember relationships. A central line depicts the child, and distances along the line depict various ages from birth to the present. Various genograms, linked to the appropriate ages, represent the families with whom the child has lived. The child can use various colors to differentiate families. The central concept of the Famograph can be used successfully in eliciting, ordering, and clarifying information for anyone who has experienced a complex series of life events, which is not uncommon in adoption.

Hartman (1979) introduced the use of the Eco-Map in adoption, and strongly supports the use of the genogram. The *Eco-Map* is a method of representing the nature and extent of the interactions within a family unit and the interactions of various members with key elements of the world beyond the family. Hartman (1979) proposes its use in the assessment of families for adoption (rather than in post-adoption). It is also a useful aid in seeking information from clients, especially couples and families, who are in conflict about the involvement of various family members with various elements of their world. Prepared formats of the Eco-Map can be found in both Hartman and Bourgnignon and Watson (1987b).

Finally, the *genogram* is a technique widely used by practitioners who work from a family systems perspective. Hartman (1979) advocates its use in the assessment of families for adoption. The genogram allows the representation, using conventions and basic symbols, of the extended family system over a number of generations. It elicits, clarifies, and documents information in a readily accessible format. It is possible to include important adoption information on the genogram (such as birth parents, a relinquished child) in a way that restores the realities of the relationships of all members of one extended adoption family. Both Hartman and Bourguignon and Watson (1987b) provide a more detailed discussion on the use of genograms with adoptive families.

Assessment of Adopted Children

While all of the above applies to all members of the adoption triad, including children, some specific points need to be made in relation to the assessment of adopted children.

It is important to interview both the adoptive parents (individually and together) and other family members (as a family unit).

The child's background prior to joining the adoptive family must be taken into account, regardless of the child's age at the time of the adoption. Background information from the birth families (medical, personal, and social), as well as prenatal and birth histories, can be significant.

A multi-disciplinary approach to the assessment of the adopted child is recommended. Many adopted children experience difficulties in a number of areas, especially in education. For example, it is now well established that there is an over-representation of adopted children with Attention Deficit Disorder (Deutsch et al., 1982).

Once a therapist has completed a thorough assessment and understood the client's adoption experience, a plan of intervention can be made. We will now discuss a variety of therapeutic interventions which will assist the therapist in planning and implementing appropriate interventions to members of the extended adoption family.

Additional information about assessment as it relates specifically to birth parents, adoptive parents, and adoptees is provided in chapters 4, 5, and 6 respectively.

THERAPEUTIC INTERVENTION

The prerequisites for implementing any form of intervention are (a) a safe working relationship, in which the client feels validated (this should have been developing throughout the assessment process), and (b) a therapeutic contract with clearly stated goals. The therapist and the client will have reached an agreement as to whether or not any of the client's family will be involved at any time, and how best their involvement can be achieved. The "adoption factor" can be an additional complication in seeking the involvement of others in the therapeutic process.

Goals of Intervention

Regardless of the preferred form of post-adoption intervention, the primary goals of intervention are (a) to affirm the client's experiences and difficulties (often they feel that they are the "only ones" and they need to know that their experiences are shared by others); (b) to assist the client in clarifying issues, reaching his or her own conclusions, and making his or her own decisions in his or her own time; (c) to assist the client in dealing with externally imposed barriers (e.g., family injunctions or conflicts over the discussion of adoption matters, difficulties regarding search); and (d) to assist the client in integrating the past with the present.

Therapeutic Techniques

We have not adopted a "how to" approach in our discussion of appropriate therapeutic techniques. Rather, we provide a commentary on why we believe certain techniques are useful. We strongly advise against the use of any therapeutic technique by persons not proficient in its use.

Counseling

Many of the traditional counseling and psychotherapeutic approaches are appropriate when working with members of the extended adoption family, whether the therapist is working with the individual or a couple. It is important for the post-adoption clinician to be able to intervene at times of crisis, both from the therapeutic and practical perspectives.

Grief Work

Facilitating the mourning of a loss is frequently required when working with birth parents, adoptive parents, and adoptees. They may each have several losses to mourn at different stages of the therapeutic process. The grief work is likely to commence with the "telling of the story" phase in assessment; however, it is highly likely that additional attention must be paid to the mourning of the losses identified throughout therapy. Typically the therapist can expect intense expressions of anger and sadness. The client is likely to have many fantasies of his or her lost object, and each of these will need to be explored; eventually, the client will "let go" and move toward the realities of the situation. The therapist can use ritual and action techniques to facilitate the "letting go" process.

One of the anomalies of adoption is that often the full resolution of grief is not possible until a search and reunion is effected. A search and reunion are then normal responses to the loss incurred through the adoption process. The decision to undertake a search, however, must be the responsibility of the client; only then will it have real therapeutic value.

Assertiveness Training

There are many uses of assertiveness training when working with clients who present with adoption-related issues. The use of this technique will most likely be beneficial when a client is struggling with the decision to search, or when he or she is already in the process of searching.

A person must feel that he or she has a "right" to search before actually embarking on the search. Assertiveness training can help a client believe in his or her right to know background information. This is especially useful during the search process itself, when one is most likely to meet resistance from the establishment and significant others. It is during this process that he or she must remember his or her right to the information sought. Adoptive parents who want to gain more background information on the child can also benefit from this technique, as they, too, will meet with resistance, especially from the agency where they adopted their child. Once reunion has taken place, assertiveness training may be useful in forming and defining new relationships and setting boundaries. Assertiveness training is especially beneficial to the birth mother and father, in relation to their right to search. It will also assist the client who needs to resume taking control of his or her life and begin affecting his or her own destiny.

Problem Solving and Conflict Resolution

These techniques are useful whenever the client is faced with a decision to make or a dilemma to resolve. The therapist will enable her or him to explore all possible options and their ramifications, choose a course of action, and evaluate the possible outcomes. If the conflict is between two people, the therapist may need to extend his or her role and become a mediator. In the adoption process, there are many instances when these skills are appropriate. For example, the woman who finds herself pregnant and does not believe in abortion, the couple who have been unable to conceive a child, the adoptee who is ambivalent about searching, the reunited adoptee and birth parent who are in conflict over the parameters of their relationship.

Role Play

Any situation which elicits fear, criticism, and uncertainty as to how to proceed (there are many in the adoption field) would benefit from role play. The technique is useful for people of all ages and in many different situations. They can also rehearse their preferred way. This will increase confidence and a sense of control, and so minimize fear and uncertainty. Role playing is especially helpful in rehearsing initial contact between the adoptee and birth parent.

Guided Fantasy

This technique is very effective with clients who are in the process of searching for a birth parent or a relinquished child. The search process is typically marked by anxiety and concern about what will be found. The use of guided fantasy can help a client explore the fantasies held about the person sought and can also be beneficial in preparation for reunion. Adoptive parents may benefit from this technique as well. They may use guided imagery as a way to explore their feelings concerning the birth parents, or they may find it especially helpful when their adoptive child embarks on a search. The PACER workshop "Healing Ourselves," for birth mothers, contains a very useful script (Brown. C., A Workshop for Birth Parents, "Healing Ourselves", PACER, 1984).

Projective Techniques

Examples of projective techniques most commonly used are sand tray, art, and play. Art and play therapy are often the preferred mediums when working with children. They are especially useful when working with adopted children who are struggling to understand the meaning of their adoptive status. The sand tray is used more commonly throughout the developmental process, especially during transitional stages of life when one redefines oneself with respect to the world. These stages might include relinquishment for the birth parent, the early stages of adoptive parenthood, the realization of adoptive status for the adoptee, and at reunion.

Journal Writing

Keeping a journal through periods of rapid and significant change can be a useful adjunct to the more formal therapeutic process. It assists the client in understanding his or her emotional and behavioral responses and to clarify his or her thinking. It can also be reassuring to the client that change and growth has indeed taken place, when mere reflecting back, without the documentation, would not be so convincing. Journal writing is especially useful when an adoptee or birth parent embarks on the search and reunion process.

Nonverbal Therapies

Many forms of predominantly nonverbal therapy (e.g., holding therapy) are being chosen by therapists in cases where children are suffering from disrupted attachments. The therapeutic goal is in the development of the child's ability to trust. Through physical contact, the therapist, rather than the child, maintains control in the context of the relationship. Anderson and Cline, in Grabe (1986), discuss such therapy in more detail.

Homework Assignments

Tasks to be undertaken by the client between sessions, as an adjunct to therapy, will encourage the client to assume more responsibility (and control) in the process of change. Because of control issues in adoption, homework assignments can have a profound influence. Tasks might include seeking information from family members or agencies to complete gaps in their knowledge, confronting persons with whom the client has "unfinished business," or acting on a decision made in therapy.

Family Therapy

Many adoption-related issues and difficulties are effectively dealt with when family therapy techniques are used. Many of the issues have implications for all family members. A thorough understanding of family systems and ways of intervening in the dysfunctional family system are required. Examples of issues which lend themselves to such intervention are:
- secrecy and denial (all triad members);
- dysfunctional communication (often a consequence of secrecy and denial);
- marital tension because of unresolved infertility and adoption-decision issues;
- overprotectiveness of child by parents (birth parents and adoptive parents);
- inhibited parenting (birth parents and adoptive parents);
- sense of belonging/family identity (adolescent adoptee);
- dealing with the issue of difference (adoptive families and adoptees);
- fear of rejection, heightened by search (all triad members); and
- family boundary issues, heightened by search and reunion (all triad members).

Therapeutic Support Groups

Group therapy programs for triad members (separate or mixed) are powerful modes of intervention. They provide a supportive and normative environment in which the group members can explore personal and common concerns, and constitute a powerful way of redressing the feelings of loneliness and isolation. The groups are facilitated by a therapist, who may or may not be a member of the triad. Examples of therapeutic support groups are those for adoptees and birth parents who are just beginning to deal with their adoption experience; for those who are searching; for adoptive parents who need to talk with their child about adoption; for adolescent adoptees in crisis and their adoptive parents.

Additional information on therapeutic support groups will be provided in chapters 4, 5, and 6.

Self-help Groups

Therapists should not overlook the therapeutic value of self-help groups (Floud, 1982); a referral to a relevant group greatly enhances the therapeutic process. Most cities have self-help groups conducted by members of the adoption triad. Write for their brochures, membership applications,

Basic Clinical Issues 43

and lists of recommended readings to hand to clients in your office. Some groups rent or sell audiovisual materials.

How can I contact and/or make a referral to an adoption self-help group? Perhaps the most direct method of locating adoption self-help groups is to consult the local telephone book under "adoption." If an adoption agency is listed, called them for the name(s) and number(s) of any adoption self-help group(s) in your area. Groups for adoptees are usually referred to as "search" groups or "search and support groups."

Self-Help Groups in the U.S.

The majority of adoption groups belong to the *American Adoption Congress* (AAC), the national umbrella organization of adoptees, birth parents, and adoptive parents. They welcome membership from and participation by professionals and agency representatives. Write the AAC for a listing of groups: P.O. Box 44040, L'Enfant Plaza Station, Washington, D.C. 20026-0040.

Another valuable resource is the *International Soundex Reunion Registry* (ISSR) (P.O. Box 2312, Carson City, Nevada 89702). ISSR accepts listings from adoptees, siblings, birth parents, and adoptive parents who are seeking to be reunited with those from whom they were separated through adoption. ISSR has established a medical information registry to receive information from agencies and individuals when critical genetic information is discovered. ISSR also maintains up to date listings of adoption self-help groups in the United States.

The North American Council on Adoptable Children (NACAC), P.O. Box 14808, Minneapolis, MN 55414, provides support and advocacy for families who adopt children with special needs, and is a source of information regarding adoptive parent support groups in the United States and Canada.

OURS, Ins., 3307 Highway 100 North, Suite 203 Minneapolis, MN 55422, provides support for adoptive parents and has chapters throughout the United States.

Resolve, Inc., P.O. Box 474, Belmont, MA 02178, is a network of local support groups for infertile couples and has chapters across the United States.

Concerned United Birthparents, Inc. (CUB, Inc. 2000 Walker Street, Des Moines, IA 50317) is a national, nonprofit organization providing support and advocacy primarily for birth parents, but its membership includes all members of the adoption triad as well as professionals.

Self-Help Groups in Australia

All the Australian states have triad groups, which are mostly search and contact focused. A number are listed below.

Victoria: **Jigsaw**, Victoria, G.P.O. 5260 BB, Melbourne 30001 Vic.

New South Wales: **Adoption Triangle**, P.O. Box 156, Wentworthville, 2145, N.S.W.

South Australia: **Jigsaw**, S.A., 30 Alexandra Avenue, Rose Park, 5067, S.A.

Queensland: **Jigsaw**, Queensland, P.O. Box 36, Earlville, 4870 QLD

Tasmania: **Jigsaw Tasmania**, P.O. Box 445, Devonport, 7310 TAS and G.P.O. Box 989K, Hobart, 7001

Northern Territory: Representative Mrs. Jan Horvath, 26 Brayshaw Cres., Millner, Darwin, 5792 N.T.

Western Australia: **Adoption Jigsaw** W.A. Inc., P.O. Box 252, Hillarys 6025. W.A.

There are many adoptive parent organizations in Australia; they are state or territory (Northern Territory and Australian Capital Territory) based and are either broad based groups or more focused on special needs adoption and inter-country adoption. Readers should check their local telephone directory under Adoptive Parent Association. For inter-country adoptions, the organizations are:

- Australians Aiding Children., in South Australia
- Australian Society for Intercountry Aid-Children (ASIAC) in New South Wales and Victoria; and
- Australia for Children Society, Inc., in West Australia

The Association for Relinquishing Mothers (ARMS) provides support and advocacy for birth parents throughout Australia. ARMS has groups in most states.

- ARMS: care of 3 Islington Crescent, Greenacre, 2190, New South Wales;
- ARMS; P.O. Box 60, Tuart Hill, 6060; West Australia;
- ARMS; care of 7 Davies Street, Malvern East, 3144 Victoria.

Self-Help Groups in New Zealand

In New Zealand, self-help groups are locally based. For details of local search and contact groups, contact Jigsaw Inc., P.O. Box 28-037 Remuera, Auckland, New Zealand. There is also a birth mothers support group: Aotearoa Birth Mothers Support Group, P.O. Box 5479, Wellesley Street, Auckland, New Zealand. For further enquiries, including information about local adoptive parent organizations, contact the Department of Social Welfare (Adoptions) Private Bag, Postal Center, Wellington, New Zealand.

Self-Help Groups in the United Kingdom

In the U.K., the major national self-help group concerned with search and contact is the National Organization for the Reunion of Child and Parent (N.O.R.C.A.P.), 3 New High Street, Headington, Oxford, England, X3 7AJ.

There are contact persons in a number of different areas of the United Kingdom.

There are also various adoptive parent groups in the United Kingdom (e.g., Parent to Parent Information on Adoption Services — P.P.I.A.S.). These are generally regionally based. Information about these groups can be obtained from local adoption agencies.

Readings

Many books and articles have been written by and for members of the adoption triad. They give personal accounts of a wide variety of adoption experiences. Reading such materials can help to minimize the client's experience of alienation and may clarify some of his or her own thoughts and feelings. The bibliography in this guidebook lists books suitable for therapists to recommend to clients. It is desirable for the therapist to read the books before making recommendations, so that she or he can assist the client in processing responses.

The following selected readings (these are fully referenced in the bibliography) are suggested as particularly appropriate to recommend to clients:

For all members of the triad:

1. Dirck Brown's *Dialogue for understanding: a handbook for Adoptive and Pre-Adoptive Parents* (Volume I). First hand accounts by adoptive parents, adoptees, and birth parents describing their lifelong adoption experience.

2. Sorosky, Baran, and Pannor's *The Adoption Triangle: Sealed or Open records: How They Affect Adoptees, Birth Parents and Adoptive Parents*. A comprehensive report, based on interviews and correspondence with adoptees, birth parents, and adoptive parents, of the effects of the reunion experience, and a critique of adoption policies with recommendations for needed changes in adoption policy and practice.

3. Rosie Snow's *Understanding Adoption, a Practical Guide* is a comprehensive review of adoption practices in Australia with an emphasis on the needs of adoption triad members.

4. Betty Jean Lifton's *Lost and Found: the Adoption Experience*. A sensitive analysis of the psychological impact of growing up adopted: the meaning of search and reunion for the adoptee, the birth parents, and the adoptive parents; and a concluding statement on the adoptee's right to know his origins.

5. Betty Jean Lifton's *Twice Born: Memories of an Adopted Daughter*. A sensitive and moving account of the author's search for her birth parents and her own identity.

6. Florence Fisher's *The Search for Anna Fisher*. A personal account of her

twenty-one year search for her birth parents by the founder of the Adoptee Liberty Movement Association (ALMA).

7. David Kirk's *Shared Fate: a Theory and Method of Adoptive Relationships*. This book changed our thinking about adoption, by describing how important it is for adoptive parents to acknowledge that their experience is basically different from that of non-adoptive families.

8. Lois Melina's *Raising Adopted Children: a Manual for Adoptive Parents*. Essential reading for adoptive and pre-adoptive parents, by an author who is herself an adoptive parent.

For birth parents:

1. Robin Winkler's and Margaret van Keppel's *Relinquishing Mothers in Adoption: Their Long-Term Adjustment*. The first comprehensive and scientific research study of relinquishing mothers, which documents that their experience is long-lasting and negative.

2. Kate Inglis's *Living Mistakes* contains first-hand moving accounts of the experience of Australian women who relinquished their children for adoption.

3. PACER's *Dialogue for understanding, Volume 2: Women's Voices* is a collection of personal statements by women (adoptees, adoptive parents, and birth parents) which provides a view of the infinite variety of adoption experiences.

For adoptive parents:

1. Lois Melina's *Raising Adopted Children: A Manual for Adoptive Parents* is an invaluable resource for both pre-adoptive and adoptive parents, packed with practical information for all aspects of adoptive parenthood. Ms. Melina's *Adopted Child* newsletter provides up to date information on topics of current interest in the adoption field.

2. Claudia Jewett's *Helping Children Cope with Separation and Loss* describes the grieving process faced by children of adoption and provides specific ways in which children can resolve their losses.

For adoptees:

1. All of the books listed above for adoptive parents, especially Lifton's *Twice born* and *Lost and found*; Fisher, *The Search for Anna Fisher*; Brown's *Dialogue for Understanding*; and Sorosky, Baran and Pannor's *The Adoption Triangle*.

For adolescent adoptees:

1. Jill Krementz's *How it Feels to be Adopted* is an appealing book of photographs of adolescent adoptees which also contains their personal statements about their feelings about being adopted.

2. Betty Jean Lifton's *I'm still me* is a fictionalized account of an adolescent girl's growing up adopted.

The following are recommended for families who adopted transracially:

1. Gill, O., & Jackson, B., *Adoption and Race: Black, Asian and Mixed*

Race Children in White Families, explores self-esteem among transracially adopted children.

2. McRoy, R., & Zurcher, L.A., *Transracial and Inracial Adoptees: the Adolescent Years,* provides insight into the experiences of blacks adopted transracially, including experience with siblings, family members, school and dating.

3. Baldwin, M.L., *An exploration of the Needs and Concerns of Caucasian Families Who Have Adopted Asian Children: A Workshop Model* presents the results of a day long workshop and provides special insights into the experience of families who adopt Asian children and the children themselves at different stages in their development.

For couples considering AID and/or surrogacy, and professionals with whom they have contact:

1. Snowden and Mitchells's *The Artificial Family* is based on information relating to more than 1000 cases where artificial insemination was requested and which have resulted in more than 400 AID babies. The book describes the reality of those experiences and the profound effects this practice has on the families involved. It is essential reading for all concerned.

2. Joseph Davis's and Dirck Brown's article in the July 1984 issue of the Western Journal of Medicine, "Artificial Insemination by Donor (AID) and the use of Surrogate Mothers," describes the negative effects of these two procedures for the families involved but especially on the child.

Chapter 4

Birth Parents

INCIDENCE

Many more women have relinquished children for adoption than most of us realize. It is conservatively estimated that one in 50 women in Western countries in 1988 will have placed a child for adoption (traditional, closed adoption) since the beginning of the twentieth century. Approximately half of these women are likely to have experienced much pain and suffering during their subsequent lives as a result of their decision to relinquish their child (Winkler & van Keppel, 1984).

The reported incidence of birth mothers who suffer long after the relinquishment appears to be low, and this is largely because of the "conspiracy of silence" and the prevalent mythology surrounding birth mothers. Adoption legislation and practice have traditionally underplayed the role of the birth parent in the adoption process. The mothers are typically encouraged to try to forget about their children, and the loss is rarely mourned. The stereoptypic image of a birth mother was one who did not care about her child. The secrecy provisions of adoption procedures and laws were not only believed to be in the best interests of the adoptee and the adoptive parents, but were also intended to preserve the honor of the birth mothers.

It is only in more recent years that birthparents have "come out" and talked publicly of their private anguish. There is also a growing body of recent research data which has supported the claims of birth parents that relinquishing a child is indeed a profound loss experience, and that this life event can have long-term deleterious results (Condon, 1986; Deykin, Campbell and Patti, 1984; Fonda, 1984; Inglis, K., 1984; McHutchison, 1986; Rynearson, 1982; and Winkler and van Keppel, 1984).

While a considerable proportion of birth fathers are not aware of their role in the adoption process (because the birth mothers chose not to or were unable to disclose such information to the fathers of their children), those who were involved also suffer. While fewer birth fathers seek professional services in an attempt to alleviate their suffering, those who do, appear to have similar experiences to the birth mothers. The information in this chapter will apply to all birth parents, unless specifically stated to be relevant to either the birth mother or the birth father.

THE DECISION TO RELINQUISH

The decision of whether or not to relinquish one's child for adoption was more often than not, the most difficult decision birth parents were ever likely to have to make. There was no easy solution to the crisis they were in, despite the fact that the decision to relinquish was in response to a life crisis at a particular time in the parent's life.

The private experience of many birth parents' as they absorb the implications of the decision is overwhelming and disruptive. They have been reluctant to convey this because of a belief that theirs is an abnormal reaction and that they are somehow more disturbed than the decision has warranted. Their experience becomes compounded by a further blow to their self-esteem with increased feelings of isolation and alienation.

BRIEF DESCRIPTION OF POST-RELINQUISHMENT PROBLEMS

The long-term disruptive effects of relinquishment experienced by birth parents place many stresses on their emotional and physical well-being; they also place great stress on their relationships with their partners, children, and with members of their families of origin.

Many of the difficulties experienced by birth parents are directly or indirectly the legacy of past social values and adoption practice. Many birth parents seek professional assistance despite feeling extremely angry, resentful, and fearful of judgmental professionals (because of their experiences around the time of relinquishment). They are fearful of having their typically poor self-images reinforced and discovering that they are especially disturbed because they haven't been able to forget about the loss of a child. Therefore, many choose to go to self-help groups rather than to professionals.

Not only do most birth parents present with a need to resolve issues directly associated with the relinquishment of their children (e.g., their sense of loss, telling others about the relinquished child, the decision to search, post-reunion difficulties), but they also can present for assistance with issues which have a more indirect association with the relinquishment (e.g., difficulties in relationships with partners, subsequent children and family of origin; poor self-esteem, disabling grief reactions). There are also problems at the time of presentation which are inextricably linked with the traumas associated with relinquishment. Examples of such problems include depression, chemical dependence, eating disorders, and anxiety/phobic states. Many are isolated and lonely people.

This chapter will consider the needs of birth parents at different life stages, and birth parent stories will be used to illustrate practice issues. Various levels of intervention will be described and the chapter will close with a reiteration of essential practice principles.

SERVICES AVAILABLE DURING THE DECISION-MAKING PERIOD

While it is recognized that the focus of this book is essentially post-adoption, the quality of support and services available to birth parents around the time they are making the decision regarding relinquishing their children will have extensive implications for their adjustment in the post-relinquishment phases. A full knowledge of the possible implications of relinquishment will assist the adoption worker to provide a comprehensive service to prospective birth parents.

The experiences of birth parents who relinquished in the past have guided the formulation of the guidelines listed below. Too frequently, birth parents have stated that they felt pressured into relinquishing their children by adoption workers (and others). They felt they were not given accurate or adequate information about alternatives to adoption, about their rights as birth parents, and about the adoption process. Almost none expected the strong emotional reactions which they experienced, and were not encouraged to actively mourn the loss of their child. Many felt incidental to the adoption process and felt the major focus of interest was with the child and adoptive family. Many received no or only minimal information about the family with whom the child was placed. Even fewer received information about the early progress of the child.

The above difficulties have resulted in additional, more complicated psychological and social difficulties than might otherwise have been expected to result from the relinquishment process. For example:
- A sense of powerlessness and betrayal that has permeated subsequent relationships, not only with professionals but also with family and friends.
- Inability to mourn the loss of their child, because they have no memories of the actual child; there was often no saying goodbye, nor memories of seeing or touching their child which would have assisted the parents to shift their experience from the realm of fantasy into the realm of reality. Denial of the experience was promoted as an effective coping strategy.
- Damaged self-esteem and a strong sense of worthlessness (complicated by

shame and guilt) resulted from the way in which their needs and experiences were ignored by members of the adoption community.

The following guidelines will assist those working with birth parents during the decision-making process.

1. Always impart clear, factual, and accurate information about adoption, the relinquishment process, its emotional implications, and other options and resources available to the parents.

2. Present them with a balanced picture of the implications of adoption, and if desired, have them meet with a range of people who can relate their personal experiences.

3. Have them understand that the decision to relinquish is likely to be one of the most difficult decisions they are ever likely to make.

4. Never give parents advice or information that may pressure their decision one way or another. Further, stress that the decision must be the responsibility of the parents themselves and one that they feel able to live with.

5. Convey to the parents that support from family and friends, and opportunities to express their feelings will greatly enhance their adjustment to their loss; if necessary, facilitate the availability of support.

6. If the parents proceed to relinquish their child for adoption, assist them to clarify their wishes regarding contact with their child. Support them in having these wishes met.

7. Ensure that a full history is taken from both birth parents (where possible); this will not only meet the primary need of supplying comprehensive information to the adoptee and the adoptive family, but it will also reinforce the importance of the role of the birth parents in the adoption process. A profile of the adoptive parents, if desired, will assist the birth parent in the adjustment process.

8. Facilitating the two-way exchange of information between the birth parents and the adoptive family on an ongoing basis will assist the birth parents to accept the reality of the existence of their child and the adoption.

9. Encouraging birth parents to leave a letter or gift for their child will further acknowledge that it is understood that the relinquishment of their child for adoption is an act of love and has been done with great care and concern.

Case Study

Karen, 20 years old, sought pre-relinquishment counseling four and one-half months into her pregnancy. She and her child's father, Peter, 22, had been in a relationship which lasted for six months. The relationship had ended six weeks before Karen discovered that she was two and one half months pregnant. Karen was a student and Peter, having just graduated, was due to commence full-time employment. Karen informed Peter of the pregnancy and that she planned to pursue adoption for their child. This was also what he wanted. Peter agreed to support Karen financially and emotionally throughout the pregnancy. Karen postponed her studies. They chose not to tell their parents (they lived quite some distance from their parents).

Throughout the pregnancy, Karen and Peter remained committed to their plan of placing their child for adoption. Karen sought and read all available literature on adoption and spoke to as many people as she possibly could (both professionals and members of the adoption triad). Karen approached this task in a methodical manner; she insisted that she had made her decision, but needed to know what she was letting herself in for. Karen considered all forms of adoption (closed, semi-open, and open). She took part in a prenatal support group. She maintained contact, however intermittent, with Peter, and also took some part-time work, which boosted her income and provided her with another interest and a distraction.

Peter chose not to attend counseling; Karen, however, used counseling to seek information, and to discuss her predicament and the implications of her decision for her, for Peter and for the baby. She did not however, waiver from her resolve to place her baby for adoption. Lastly, Karen chose in counseling to consider her relationship with her parents and her reluctance to tell them about her pregnancy and adoption plan. Karen was very fearful of her parent's rejection, and she explored the reasons for her fears and the implications of not telling them. Eventually, she changed her mind, and decided to tell her parents when she was seven months pregnant. Her fears proved to be unfounded; her parents were supportive and caring, and distressed that she had isolated herself for so long. Karen's mother took leave from her work and came to be with Karen for three weeks. She was not able to stay for the delivery, but she did assist Karen with her prenatal preparations and was very supportive. Her parents offered her on-going support and financial assistance if she were to decide against adoption. Karen, however, remained resolute in her decision.

Karen decided on a traditional closed adoption. She believed that a semi-open or open adoption would mean a commitment that she was unsure she could keep, in the long run. Peter also preferred a closed adoption.

Karen had a long and difficult labor and delivery. She spent a lot of time with her baby in the hospital. After discharge, Karen was not ready to sign the adoption consent form, so her baby went to a pre-adoptive foster home. She visited the baby often, and at three weeks, when she felt ready to separate and say "goodbye," she signed the adoption consent form.

During the revocation period, Karen visited her baby often. Peter visited with her on one occasion. Karen was depressed and anxious throughout the four weeks; however, she did not waiver, instead seeking additional support and contact with people she expected would validate her decision.

The revocation period expired. Peter and Karen acknowledged its passing by spending some quiet times together, and by preparing themselves to move into the next phase of their lives. The baby was placed with adoptive parents. Karen received non-identifying information and photographs, then returned home to be with her family until she could resume her studies.

IMMEDIATE POST-RELINQUISHMENT PERIOD

In the immediate post-relinquishment period, the birth mother must attempt to reconcile the implications of her decision, adjust to the loss (physically, emotionally and cognitively), and must face the many other events and stressors that have taken place in her life in the period leading up to the relinquishment. It is indeed a period of heightened vulnerability and confusion, compounded with an urgency, for many, to have their lives return to normal.

For most women, pregnancy and childbirth are universally recognized as physically, emotionally and socially stressful events, requiring a substantial period of readjustment.

Most women have children in the context of a loving and stable relationship, with the abundant support and approval of family, friends, and society. This is not the case for most birth mothers. Some do have the support and involvement of their child's father, and perhaps of their family, but they are essentially alienated from friends and the wider community.

The loss of a child through death is generally accepted to be a very tragic event for parents and family, and is typically followed by traumatic and complicated grief reactions. The loss of a child through relinquishment is similarly, for many, a very disruptive event for the mother and father and those close to them. Their emotional reactions resemble the typical grief reactions, often complicated by the birth parents' need to "suffer in silence" and to mourn the peculiar loss of their child, lost to themselves but a source of great joy and happiness to others. Some birth parents also experience great ambivalence; while the decision to relinquish their child has relieved them to pursue other life goals besides parenting at that point in time, they nonetheless experience much grief, anguish, and uncertainty. Research results indicate that the relinquishment of a child is indeed the most stressful life event most birth mothers had ever experienced (Winkler & van Keppel, 1984).

Pregnancy and relinquishment are not the only stresses experienced by birth mothers. Associated features of the relinquishment process are also inherently stressful. Many mothers have felt that they had to move to another town or city in order to avoid embarrassment to themselves and their family. Some may also have moved in order to avoid family pressure (anticipated or actual). Those who did not move may have had to endure considerable family pressure or ostracism. Feelings of loneliness, isolation, and alienation are frequently experienced. Many birth mothers also leave their regular employment and suffer dislocation, reduction in income, reduced social contacts, and a diminished sense of self-worth following withdrawal from the workforce.

Research data suggests that both the number of stresses and the magnitude of adjustment required by additional concurrent stresses or crises (e.g., change of residence, ill health, loss of income) will affect a person's adjustment to the original stressor (Andrews, Tennant, Hewson & Vaillant, 1978; Brown & Harris, 1978).

As stated above, birth mothers do experience typical grief reactions in the period after the relinquishment. The features of grief reactions are well documented, and can be summarized as follows: (a) somatic complaints (e.g., loss of appetite and sleep disturbances); (b) inappropriate cognitions (e.g., unrealistic thoughts and fantasies about the relinquished child); (c) wide variety of emotional responses (e.g., guilt, anger, despair, sadness); and (d) disturbed behavior (e.g., apathy, social withdrawal, compulsive overactivity).

Many birthmothers have reported extended periods of depression, suicidal feelings, anxiety, alcohol and drug abuse, numbness, and poor physical health immediately following the relinquishment of their child. In many instances, the birth mothers didn't necessarily attribute these physical and emotional disturbances to the loss of their child, primarily because they had been led to expect that they would not suffer, and that if they did it would be short-lived. Others fought hard to forget or deny their relinquishment, but nonetheless experienced such disturbances.

INTERVENTION

It is important that practitioners appreciate the nature and extent of the crises and changes that confront birth parents during the relinquishment process. The primary task of the immediate post-relinquishment period is to assist birth parents in understanding the specific nature of the changes they must address. In addition, it is important to provide support, to assist the birth parents in resolving conflicts and making decisions in accordance with their own needs and wishes, and to "normalize" their emotional reactions by providing reassurance and information about normal reactions to loss and other stressful life events.

Be mindful of the possibility of emotional and physical disturbances which the birth mother may not directly attribute to the loss of her child, or may dismiss as being transient or insignificant. Such disturbances must be treated as being indicative of the birth mother's need to mourn the loss of her child, express her many thoughts and feelings about other significant persons or events, and reconcile her current circumstances. Many a birth mother's disturbance is exacerbated by the fact that the reality of her loss did not match her expectations (e.g., degree of attachment to the child).

In order to facilitate this adjustment process we suggest that the worker:

Be available and accessible to the birth mother. Spend as much time with her as is necessary; this may be considerably longer than the conventional one-hour appointment.

Be non-judgmental, attentive, and open. Make sure you are ready to accept whatever thoughts or feelings the birth mother needs to express.

Encourage and facilitate the expression of feelings.

Provide reassurance. Many birth mothers are very frightened about the intensity and range of their feelings. They need to know that such reactions are not uncommon, and are not indications of loss of control or "craziness."

Be aware of your own limitations. Secondary disburbances (e.g., alcohol dependence) may develop which you do not have the expertise to address. When a referral is necessary, it is essential that the worker convey the importance of the relinquishment experience and, if necessary (or requested) remain involved in order to provide continued support and counseling.

Provide or facilitate practical assistance. This may include a place to recuperate, accomodations, and employment.

Remind the birth mother that support and assistance are available at any time in the future, should she require them. It is likely that there will be periods or events in the birth mother's subsequent life (e.g., birth of other children, anniversary of the relinquished child's birth, and so forth) that may trigger further emotional or physical disturbance. Birth parents should be advised that there could be difficult times, and that it is desirable to seek support and assistance before the reactions become too problematic.

Suggest a support group to the birth mother. A support or self-help group may be of interest and benefit to her, especially if she has expressed an interest in meeting other birth mothers.

Maintain friendly contact. Specifically, there should be one contact sometime after the more regular contacts have dissipated. The need for support, reassurance, and friendship exist long after the crisis is over. It is also possible that the birth mother is still experiencing periods of distress, but is reluctant to bother the adoption worker. Such contact will provide an additional opportunity to facilitate the adjustment process.

Case Study

Jenny, 21, is a beautician. She delivered and placed her baby for adoption around the time of her 18th birthday. Her relationship with her child's father, Chris, ended midway through the pregnancy. Although Jenny and Chris were very fond of each other, their relationship was not strong enough to survive the crisis of the pregnancy. Jenny felt very unsupported by Chris; Chris, in turn, was very hurt by Jenny's withdrawal from him. Chris favored an adoption decision, while Jenny, who had received a lot of support from her parents, was ambivalent about adoption. She sought counseling during the last trimester of her pregnancy, and maintained regular contact with the pregnancy counselor for the next four months. Jenny did not make a final adoption decision until ten days after the birth. She had a lot of contact with the baby during those ten days. Chris saw the baby twice.

Jenny returned to work three weeks after the birth, (one week after she signed the adoption consent form. At that time, she felt that she had recovered from both the delivery and the relinquishment and was eager to resume her life. Six weeks after the birth, Jenny became ill (kidney infection and minor gynecological complications) and was required to take time off from her work. As Jenny's health improved, she returned to the pregnancy counselor — "just" to talk and to see if the counselor had heard anything about the baby. However, Jenny soon broke down and became very distraught. She went through many of the usual grief reactions (guilt, sadness, anger, confusion). For the next three weeks she had frequent contact with the counselor and very actively mourned the loss of her baby. She spoke with other birth mothers during this time and formed a friendship with one of them, which has continued for the past three years.

Jenny and the pregnancy counselor now keep in touch on an intermittent basis; contact is mostly initiated by Jenny, when she needs to talk or needs to be with someone who understands. Jenny is now leading a full and satisfying life. She recently commented that she feels a lot of pain for those women who do not have anyone to talk to about their baby and who have "to keep the lid on things, because the price is just too great."

SERVICES AVAILABLE DURING THE POST-RELINQUISHMENT PERIOD

This period refers, in the main, to the birth parent's life subsequent to the relinquishment experience — i.e., once the crisis has dissipated and it is assumed that the birth parents have gone on with the business of living their lives.

Many of the difficulties experienced by birth parents are directly or indirectly the legacy of past practice. Many feel extremely angry and resentful toward the agency or personnel with whom they had contact during the relinquishment process. For this reason, it is common for birth parents to seek counseling from an agency other than the one that was involved in the adoption. They may, however, return to the original agency to seek information or to place themselves on the agency's contact register if one exists.

Providing services post-relinquishment to birth parents is a complex matter. Certain *prerequisites* for any worker are (a) a thorough understanding of the relinquishment process; (b) a comprehensive knowledge of the range of experiences birth parents may have endured in the past; and (c) a realization of the powerful impact relinquishment can have throughout the birth parent's lives.

Experience has taught us to expect anything, and to be creative in our service delivery. Birth parents are understandably fearful of judgmental professionals, of having their typically poor self-image reinforced, and of discovering that they are "crazy" because they haven't been able to forget about the loss of their child. Often it is necessary to go overboard to be nonjudgmental and accepting, reassuring them that their current difficulties are very understandable given their earlier experiences.

Procedural Matters

Birth parents need reassurance that the nature of counseling is completely confidential. It is unwise to assume that they will take confidentiality for granted.

Many birth parents either cancel appointments at late notice or fail to attend without canceling, because they feel threatened and anxious about facing the very painful issues associated with their relinquishment. It is necessary to be patient and accommodating so that birth parents will eventually receive the support and assistance they require.

Many birth parents have not told their current partners or family members about their relinquishment. For this reason, it is especially unwise to leave telephone messages, and it is sometimes necessary to try to accommodate difficult arrangements (e.g., awkward appointment times).

The conventional hour-long (or 50-minute) session often needs to be stretched, especially during the early stages of contact. Many birthparents seeking professional assistance will never have talked of their experience; they are relating their story for the first time. It is often very difficult for them to get started. When they do get started, the retelling is so powerful and upsetting that much time and care must be given to contracting and closure, necessitating a longer session. In addition, birth parents may appear to be seeking information only, but may in truth be deciding whether or not they want to return for further assistance. They may also be concerned that the information they will receive, which they may act on, will trigger other issues for them. Similarly, a birth parent who receives counseling regarding one concern may later return to consider another. Practitioners must make it possible for birth parents to have continuing contact if they wish.

Birth parents seek therapy, counseling, information, or assistance from agencies for a multitude of reasons either directly or indirectly related to the loss of their child.

While some agencies may offer group programs as a mode of intervention, services to individual clients must be tailored to meet their individual needs. Counseling and therapy may involve the birth parent's partner or family if necessary.

Post-Relinquishment Crisis

Certain events in the lives of birth parents tend to trigger an emotional upheaval which is directly or indirectly related to their relinquishment experience. Sometimes the upheaval will dissipate, only to recur following another trigger event. At some point, when the birth parents' usual coping strategies are no longer effective, they will seek support or counseling and therapy. For others, the final push that results in seeking assistance may simply be a growing recognition that the pain has not dissipated significantly since the relinquishment.

Common Trigger Events

The relinquished child's birthday, or the anniversary of the relinquishment. An especially difficult time might be when the child reaches the age of majority. Depending on the state laws regarding access to information, the age of majority also means that the relinquished child may seek contact with the birth parents. This milestone often causes birthparents to experience intense anxiety in conjunction with feelings of either hopefulness or dread.

The formation of new relationships. Many birth mothers have felt very troubled in relationships they formed with men subsequent to the relinquishment. Issues such as trust, intimacy, sexuality, self-esteem, and possessiveness created new difficulties. Some were desperate to have another child and chose a new partner in great haste and with little care. Some felt so poorly about themselves they chose partners consistent with their poor self-image and consequently suffered from physical and sexual abuse. Others, harboring the secret of their relinquishment for fear of rejection, avoided real intimacy with their partners and were continually anxious that their partners would somehow find out. Some were never able to trust anyone enough to form new stable and loving relationships. When birth mothers become aware of this pattern, they often seek professional assistance.

The birth of subsequent children. It may not necessarily be with the birth of the birth mother's second child, but at some other time there is a realization that the relinquished child has not been replaced — cannot be replaced — and is gone, apparently, forever. Other birth mothers may experience considerble difficulty in forming strong attachments to their child (ren) in fear of losing them also; alternatively, they may be possessive and overprotective. Some birth mothers choose never to have other children; this may be because of a fear of reawakening of the emotional trauma of relinquishment, or a fear that other children will diminish the importance of the relinquished child in their lives.

The death of the parents of birth parents. The loss of a birth parent's parent can trigger a very complicated grief reaction where there were unresolved matters associated with the relinquishment. Alternatively, the death may mean that the birth parent now feels free to talk about their experiences and perhaps search for their child.

The element of publicity. In recent years adoption has become much more of a public issue. There are frequent stories on the need for law reform, of people searching and reunited. Some birth parents may have a strong identification with, or reaction to, some particular news story, and it may result in them making contact with a group or agency for some reason. Some respond to the news of the death of an adopted child.

Whatever the trigger event, it is important that the meaning of this "final push" in seeking assistance be established and addressed. It is also highly likely that they will want to pursue other issues related to their relinquishment experience.

An increasing proportion of birth parents seek assistance because of a growing need to address certain difficulties in their life, either directly or indirectly related to the relinquishment. The growing need is not necessarily the result of any trigger event.

Reasons for seeking assistance

Disabling grief reactions. As has been explained earlier, many birth parents continue to experience disturbing grief reactions long after they relinquish their child for adoption. Some may experience more obvious signs of grief — for example, periods of being overwhelmed by anger, sadness, fear, guilt, preoccupation with the relinquished child, and a compulsion to search. The compulsion to search is often well planned and executed; frequently, however, it is haphazard and ineffectual. Other birth parents may experience other forms of dysfunction which are less obviously related to the loss of a child. Examples of such dysfunctions are depression, anxiety or phobic states, and substance abuse.

Difficulties in life complicated by the relinquishment. These may include marital discord, conflict with parents (where the birth mother still harbors considerable resentment, anger and guilt toward her parents for their part in the relinquishment), or difficulty in forming enduring relationships.

Low self esteem. Guilt and shame have contributed to the erosion of the birth parent's self-esteem. Some have never been able to view their predicament in any way other than disgraceful. Others, after having established some distance in time to the relinquishment, have come to believe that they have failed their child as a parent; birth fathers may feel that they failed to provide support to the mother of their child, and may continue to feel poorly about themselves. Birth parents rarely speak of their experience; as a result, there are few validating experiences for them. Many birth parents have gone on to experience other negative life experiences, reinforcing their shattered view of themselves.

Sense of betrayal. This is more frequently experienced by birth mothers than birth fathers. Much of the anger, hurt, and despair results from a feeling of betrayal by the significant people in the birth mother's life around the time of relinquishment (e.g., child's father, parents, adoption workers).

Difficulties in discussing the relinquishment: It is common for many birth parents to experience extreme difficulties in discussing their relinquishment. This is not difficult to understand when you recall that for many years they believed that their experiences carried taboo status and that they were advised to forget the child and get on with their lives. Many birth mothers appear to be emotionally and cognitively unable to talk about the child and the relinquishment. Some birth mothers have never discussed this significant life event with anyone prior to seeking assistance. Regardless of the length of time that has lapsed since the relinquishment, the pain can be very profound in the retelling, and may not significantly dissipate with subsequent retelling. Forgetting or confusing certain aspects of the relinquishment only serves to reinforce the "unreality" of their experience. For many reasons (e.g., fear of critical judgment and ostracism, injunctions from family members not to speak of the relinquishment), some birth parents have not told their partner or subsequent children of the relinquished child.

Parenting subsequent children. The nature of the difficulties will vary from birth mother to birth mother, depending on their earlier experiences and their more current experiences. The birth of the next child may be especially difficult for those mothers who were expecting the child to be a "replacement child" for the one they relinquished. Many birth mothers believe that the relinquishment proved them unable and unfit to be mothers. Others are overprotective of their other children; still others have difficulty forming close bonds with their children, because of a fear that they will lose them.

Loneliness and social anxiety: Such problems are usually associated with poor self-esteem and an inability to discuss the relinquishment experience. This results in birth mothers experiencing social isolation, difficulties in mixing freely with people, and a lack of personal and social support.

Searching. Birth parents may seek advice and support in searching for their child. These requests for assistance can range from making the decision to search or not to search, to providing support and counseling during the search itself, to the reunion and beyond.

With regard to reunions, it is important that birth parents (and indeed all parties) prepare for contact. The following must be discussed:
- Unrealistic expectations
- Fears of rejection
- Rights and responsibilities
- Implications for the adoptee and the adoptive parents
- Current family attitudes
- Frustration
- Appropriateness of the search
- Motivation
- Sense of urgency
- Implications for other family members (partners, parents, other children). Therapeutic assistance may be required once a reunion has taken place.

Interventions

While the adoption worker must work creatively in addressing the individual needs of the birth parents and, in so doing, utilize a broad range of clinical skills and therapeutic modes, the following interventions are used more frequently than others, and have been adapted to accomodate the special needs of birth parents.

Grief Work

In order to provide appropriate therapeutic interventions to assist birth parents grieving for their lost children, one must possess a thorough understanding of how the relinquishment process affects the grief response.

Although the specific nature of grief counseling may vary from birth parent to birth parent and between workers, we suggest that the process be facilitated by addressing certain tasks. They should be addressed in the approximate order that they are considered below.

Validate the birth parent's experiences and needs. Provide information about the experiences of other birth parents and about the nature of grief. Such information will allow the birth parent to feel "normal" by confirming the appropriateness of their response, and it will allow them to grieve and express their feelings.

Ascertain the nature of unconditional support available to the birth parent. Identify people who will be available to them to listen when they have a need to talk and express their feelings, and will be able to provide comfort and reassurance. Help the birth parent mobilize the support potentially available to her or him.

Reconstruct the entire relinquishment experience. Begin prior to conception and continue to the present day. This is an extension of the "telling the story" phase in assessment. Consider:
- personal circumstances around time of conception (employment, friends,)
- relationship with child's father or mother
- family circumstances around the time of conception
- finding out about the pregnancy
- having the pregnancy confirmed
- telling significant others
- reactions of others
- the decision to relinquish
- physical health and the experience of being pregnant
- feelings about being pregnant and feelings toward the unborn child
- hopes, fantasies during pregnancy
- fears during pregnancy
- nature and quality of professional help (e.g., doctors, social workers, and so forth)

- preparation for birth
- birth experience (e.g., duration of experience, of labor, actual delivery, contact with the child, support and assistance from those present)
- hospital experiences
- leaving the hospital
- signing the consent to adoption forms
- reactions of significant others around this time
- coping with the physical changes
- coping with the emotional impact of relinquishment
- reestablishing normal life (employment, accommodations, friends)
- relationship with child's father or mother around this time
- relationships with family
- forming new relationships
- marriage
- having more children
- coping with anniversaries and other significant dates or events.

It is possible that there will be some gaps or uncertainties as the story evolves. Encourage the birth parent to seek out information to either fill the gaps or clarify the uncertainties. It is important that the therapist does not, however unintentionally, collude with the birth parent in avoiding especially painful aspects of the experience, or in continuing to deny certain aspects. The reconstruction of the relinquishment experience will facilitate the expression of much feeling; in particular, sadness, anger, and shame. Expect, accept, and encourage the full expression of such emotion.

Reexamine the birth parent's decision to relinquish the child. As a result of the emotional aftermath of the relinquishment experience, many birth parents experience strong regrets about their decision and believe that they could have decided otherwise and kept the child. Allow the birth parent an opportunity to address these unresolved feelings of regret.

In addition to the loss of the child through the relinquishment experience, birth parents typically experience concomitant losses; these, too, are rarely mourned. It is necessary to facilitate the mourning and resolution of these losses. Some of the more common losses are (a) loss of control over one's life; (b) loss of self-respect; (c) loss of family support, approval, and sense of belonging; and (d) loss of career opportunities.

The therapist should encourage the birth parent to talk about how these losses occurred, the experience at the time, and how they have affected her life since, and express the feelings that are aroused. Talking and the expression of feeling frequently helps the birth parent to gain clarity and a deeper understanding of the role of these losses in her life. They will be in a more advantageous position to resolve some of the difficulties that have ensued.

Focus on the relinquished child in considerable detail. Many birth parents still have an image of the child as a baby, and they should be assisted to begin to view the relinquished child in a manner consistent with his/her current age. Relevant aspects of the child's development and current functioning need to be explained. Assist the birth parent with developing an image of their child as she or he moves through life (e.g., at school or work, fashions, values). If the birth parent did not name the child at birth, they can be encouraged to do so, or "adopt" the name the child became known by prior to the adoption (obtainable from the agency). This assists in the formation of the image of the child as a person with an identity and life of his or her own.

Find positive associations. In addition to the positive feelings associated with the relinquished child, it is suggested that other aspects of the relinquishment experience may also hold positive feelings. For example, many birth parents, in hindsight, see it as a time of "growing up," or rapid maturing. Some developed very strong friendships or functioned independently from their family for the first time in their life. These possible aspects of the relinquishment experience need to be valued and appreciated, rather than dismissed.

Come to a resolution. It is a widely held belief that the birth parent loss is irresolvable until the parent meets his or her child again (Inglis, 1984; Shawyer, 1979; Silverman, 1987). To the contrary, all the issues related to the experience of search and reunion can be appropriately explored toward the end of grief counseling. Examples of such issues are the decision to search or not to search; seeking non-identifying or identifying information; placing name and other details on contact register; and expectations regarding contact. Some birth parents, on the other hand, do not wish to actively search for their child or in fact to be reunited. They will need to feel comfortable with this decision.

Finally, the grieving of many birth parents is greatly facilitated by their meeting other birth parents, either through a support and therapy group or by joining a self-help group such as Concerned United Birth Parents (CUB) in the United States or Association of Relinquishing Mothers (ARMS) in Australia. Birth parents find great therapeutic value in the shared experience, mutual understanding, and reassurance that their own experience and reaction were not irrational but commonplace. In the process of mourning the loss of their relinquished child, many birth parents will also deal with, or begin to deal with associated issues such as self-esteem, telling others, and searching and contact.

Self-esteem
Birth parents typically suffer from low self-esteem. An important goal of

therapy, therefore, is for them to reappraise their view of themselves, and so enhance the way they feel about themselves. Self-esteem has a direct effect on one's experience, well-being, and ability to enjoy satisfactory social relationships. Low self-esteem is the result of a combination of several factors:

Rejection. Many birth parents have suffered rejection by significant people in their lives. This has reinforced their low self-esteem. While such treatment has been overt in many instances, it has also been covert (e.g., "a family secret," referring to the relinquishment as "something we don't talk about").

Regret. Many birth parents are critical of themselves because they not only transgressed society's moral codes (about sexual behavior and parenthood) but succumbed to the pressures of others and made a decision they came to regret. The birth parents may also believe that their decision may not have been in the best interests of the child.

Unresolved grief experience. This will complicate feelings of low self-esteem: not only because the birth parents feel unhappy much of the time, but because they feel they should have "gotten over" their loss. This, in turn, alienates them from others, and they receive little feedback from others that they are worthwhile and valued persons.

Therapeutic strategies for enhancing the self-esteem of birth parents have largely developed from the cognitive–behavioral approaches to self-esteem, assertion, and depression. From our clinical experience, we have found that the following strategies are effective.

1. Encourage the birth parent to question the right of others to be so condemning in their attitudes.
2. If necessary, raise questions with the birth parent such as, "why do you think your partner is so attracted to you?" or "what could your best friend possibly see in you?" These questions can cause the birth parent to reflect on her positive attributes. It is the right of every person to consider themselves important, to have an equal status with fellow human beings and to carry themselves with dignity. Assertive behavior will ensure that birth parents will receive the respect they deserve.
3. Have the birth parent reflect on the circumstances around the time of relinquishment, and the decision to relinquish. In this context have him or her justify his or her guilt, poor self-image, and lack of rights. In the absence of any justification (which is likely), she or he can view the relinquishment experiences and herself or himself less punitively and more realistically.

4. Guided imagery is a useful adjunct to the development of self-esteem. It can be relaxing, pleasant and powerful. It is primarily used to encourage the birth parent to view him or herself differently. The PACER workshop for birth parents, "Healing Ourselves" (1984) provides an exercise in guided imagery or visualization that has been used successfully on many occasions.
5. Encourage the birth parent to engage in activities which result in both "mastery" and "pleasure," so that they can enjoy themselves and experience satisfaction. Through repeated activities, the birth parents become more oriented toward their present life now and current self-worth. Their view of themselves is no longer totally contingent on their behavior in former years.

Finally, poor self-esteem is very typical of the problems experienced by birth parents. In many instances, it has contributed to secondary problems such as depression, phobic disorders (especially agoraphobia), obesity, and alcohol and drug abuse.

Telling Others

Many birth parents seek counseling at a time when they realize they no longer can or no longer wish to keep their relinquishment experience a secret from the people in their lives. The necessity to tell (partner, parents, children) often raises complex emotional difficulties, usually associated with unresolved grief and a fear of rejection.

The "secret of relinquishment" is a disruptive force in otherwise intimate or significant relationships. It encourages the proliferation of deceitful stories, usually strung together rather precariously, and the birth parent is in continual fear of being found out. The mere fact of having to maintain a "web of deceit," for whatever reason, strengthens the feelings of guilt and poor self-esteem of the birth parent. Usually where a secret exists family members are aware that there is something "not quite right." This not only creates tensions but also damages the trust that is vital for open and honest relationships.

Have the birth parent consider both the positive and negative consequences of maintaining the secret. Explore their reservations about "telling." These are likely to be associated with a fear of rejection, which will have its origins in earlier experiences.

Have the birth parent consider her or his reasons for wanting to "tell" and what he or she hopes to gain. The current reality should be assessed; it may be that the risk of possible negative outcomes outweigh the gains that might be achieved by "telling."

Consider how he or she wishes to convey the information. The parent will not wish to undermine her or his integrity and dignity and pave the way for further rejection and criticism. If the secret is told in a manner which maintains their dignity and self-respect, it is more likely to be responded to accordingly. Rehearsal and role playing are appropriate techniques here.

Standard therapeutic procedures are appropriate when dealing with the secondary difficulties that can be experienced by birth parents (e.g., depression, anxiety, phobic states, chemical dependency, eating disorders). A referral to a therapist who is able to deal with these problems *and* acknowledge the importance of the relinquishment experience can be considered.

The value of the therapeutic support groups (agency-facilitated) and self-help groups (for birth parents only or for all triad members) cannot be overstated. The type of group experience will depend on the personality and needs of the birth parent.

Case Study

Susan, 44, became pregnant at the age of 23. She was single at the time, but the pregnancy occurred in the context of a loving and stable relationship. She relinquished her daughter soon after birth. Susan came from a very moralistic family and thought they could not and would not accept her being unmarried and pregnant. She believed she had no option but to place her child for adoption; she was afraid to broach the subject of marriage and didn't tell her child's father of the pregnancy. At four months, Susan ended the relationship, resigned from her teaching job, and went out of state. She obtained live-in employment with a family, and stayed away until after the birth and the adoption formalities were complete.

However, during the final stages of her pregnancy, Susan reconsidered her adoption decision. In seeking assistance, she was continually frustrated, and disappointed, and eventually felt railroaded into relinquishment. Susan recalls an overwhelming sense of powerlessness. Following the birth and relinquishment, Susan returned to her home state. For the first six months, Susan felt very unhappy and was contemplating getting pregnant again. She eventually formed a stable relationship with a man with whom she felt safe.

Susan sought therapy after she had had a devastating experience of being powerless all over again. She was overcome by the memories and feelings associated with her relinquishment; she became very angry, anxious, and withdrawn, and felt "out of control."

In therapy, Susan was assisted in particular by grief work and assertiveness training. She gained a new perspective on the actions of the adoption worker who had failed to assist her when she was reconsidering, and slowly her personal power returned. Susan also joined a therapeutic support group, and later a self-help group. She has gained greatly from her membership in both types of groups.

GUIDING PRINCIPLES FOR THERAPY WITH THE BIRTH PARENT

In conclusion, there are certain features of the birth parent's experience which necessitate special consideration in the provision of services.

1. The central focus of therapy is the relinquishment experience. Many birth parents have commented that previous consultations with therapists have been of limited value because the relinquishment experience was not treated with the significance required.
2. Reconstruct the birth parent's story in detail, from prior to the relinquishment to the present. This reconstruction will not only include events, but also associated feelings and thoughts.
3. Take the birth parents through their experience with compassion and interest. Avoid superficiality. Expect and accommodate the expression of intense feelings.
4. Work at the pace set by the birth parent. It is important that sufficient time is available, especially in the initial sessions, for a substantial part of the birth parent's story to be told, as well as for closure.
5. It may be necessary to reconsider the story of the relinquishment, or parts of it, on subsequent occasions.
6. Assess the level of the birth parent's self-esteem and be mindful of the need to build self-esteem using formal and informal strategies.

Chapter 5
Adoptive Parents

In this chapter we discuss the tasks of adoptive parents. Adoptive parenting is inherently different from non-adoptive parenting. We present these differences and tasks within the context of the adoptee's developmental stages, since the adoptive family's ability to respond to such issues parallels the maturation of the adoptee.

The extent to which adoptive parents acknowledge, respond to, and resolve these special adoption-related tasks (Brokzinsky, 1986; Kirk, 1984) will determine the adoptive family's adjustment to the adoption experience.

Joanne Small (1987) describes the adoptive family as follows:

> Adoptive families are structured out of loss. Infertile couples lose the fullfillment reproduction normally brings, as well as the fantasy of biological reproduction. This is a loss of both status and self-esteem at a time when it seems that all other adults can reproduce. For all adoptive parents there is a symbolic loss, in that the child they adopt can never be the child they would have produced biologically. The emotional effects of infertility are often devastating to the couple. When poorly resolved, these losses can have potentially negative effects upon adoptive family structure... With each loss comes a need to grieve and to work through the associated pain and suffering. Both parents and children of adoption lack the opportunity to grieve their losses because those losses have largely gone unrecognized by themselves and others. Instead, children of adoption and their parents are caught in another myth: that adoption is a panacea (Small, pp. 35,36).

TASKS OF ADOPTIVE PARENTHOOD

The Pre-Adoptive Period

Infertility

Prior to arriving at the decision to adopt a child, the majority of prospective adoptive parents try many times to conceive a child of their own. During this process, they must undergo numerous medical examinations and related procedures to determine the cause of their infertility; anticipation of conception is followed by deep disappointment. This emotional seesaw can cause high levels of stress. Further tests and medication may be prescribed for years, as the couple continue to attempt to conceive a child. Some couples exhaust every medical alternative before deciding to adopt, while others make that decision earlier. In either case, the couple is now faced with the task of mourning the child they cannot have.

Similarly, couples who are advised against conception because they are at high risk of transmitting inherited conditions (e.g., Huntington's Chorea, hemophilia, sickle cell anemia) and so choose adoption must also grieve for the child they cannot have.

The importance of mourning the inability to bear one's own child is widely recognized (Brown, 1981; Derdeyn, 1980; Kraft et al., 1980; Sorosky et al., 1978; Blum, 1976; Kent & Richie, 1976). Grief resolution involves the opportunity to express one's feelings concerning the loss and having these feelings acknowledged. It is aided by knowing that support is available from others. For many infertile couples, however, such support is not available. Without the support of family, friends, or health professionals, many couples are left alone to face their pain. The intrapsychic tasks of such grief resolution include the acceptance of working through the loss of an ideal of self, the restitution of damaged body image, and an assessment of the importance of parenthood. An adaptive resolution is necessary for successful adoptive parenting (Kraft et al., 1980).

Kent and Richie (1976) describe two styles that infertile couples use to cope: (a) those couples who deny or represss their grief and decide to adopt right away, and (b) those couples who allow themselves the opportunity to grieve before making the decision to adopt.

Sorosky et al. (1978) emphasize that women who do not resolve their angry feelings prior to adoption often displace them onto the birth mother. The adoptive mother and the adoptive father may resent the birth parent's ability to have children. Prospective adoptive parents who do not resolve their own feelings of loss prior to adoption will be unable to help the adoptee cope with his or her own sense of loss. Small (1987) emphasizes that for the adoptee "adoption always means a loss of relationships with emotionally significant objects and a symbolic loss of roots, a sense of genetic identity, and a sense of connectedness" (see chapter 6).

Renne (1977) compared infertility to a death in the family and believed that it should be mourned as such. She found that feelings of shock, protest, and denial preceded successful grief resolution, and 60–70 percent of the couples applying for adoption were still experiencing these feelings. Renne found that many of these couples had not been told that their grief reactions were normal. Once these feelings were brought into awareness, most couples could work through their grief. Many adoption agencies now offer prospective adoptive parents opportunities to resolve their infertility. Attendance at an "Infertility Workshop" is sometimes a prerequisite for the placement of a child.

Motivation for adoption

Adoptive parents' motivations for adoption can have a direct bearing on the expectations (often covert) they develop for their adopted child(ren) and on the dynamics of the family. These expectations may or may not be functional. Examples of common motivations for adoption are:

1. a desire to become parents, create a family, and enjoy a full and satisfying family life, these desires being otherwise unrealisable because of infertility;
2. a desire for more children than they are able to have naturally;
3. a chance to provide a permanent family and home for a child who might otherwise have remained in institutional or temporary care;
4. a need to prove to themselves or others that they too can be parents despite their inability to conceive or carry a child to full term;
5. a response to family and social pressure to create a family, despite being unable to do so naturally;
6. a need to replace a child lost through death;
7. an opportunity to provide permanent and stable care to a child that is known to them, either through concern or a sense of responsibility.

Preparation for Adoption

The pre-adoptive period is a particularly difficult one for prospective adoptive parents. Once they have decided to adopt, for whatever reason, they are faced with various issues, which they must address. Those that are not addressed adequately can become more pressing concerns later, with implications not only for the adoptive parents, but also for the adoptee and other family members. These issues are:

- infertility (failure, loss, effect on self-esteem);
- the social stigma of adoption (attitudes about illegitimacy, someone else's child, and so forth);
- the emotional stigma of adoption — in particular, the idea that adoption can be a solution to a problem rather than the preferred means of creating a family;

- the reaction of family and friends;
- the realities of adoption — in particular, the fact that the child was born to other parents, and the need to accomodate this fact of adoption in their lives and that of the child (i.e., realistic expectations about adoptive parenthood);
- feelings toward the birth parents (fear, envy, mystery, gratitude, and so forth);
- anxiety about how secure, binding and permanent adoptive relationships really are;
- anxiety and resentment associated with the assessment of their suitability to be adoptive parents (while they have a strong need to be judged as competent parents, many find the assessment process long and intrusive);
- uncertainty (as the wait between assessment, approval and placement is long, during this time their desire for a child may oscillate as they accommodate various hopes, dreams and frustrations);
- growing anxiety about the tasks of adoptive parents (e.g., the dilemma of living with their adopted child "as if" it were born to them, having to tell their child of their adoption and, at the same time, helping the child live with that fact).

After trying for some time to conceive a child of their own, they must submit (if they choose an agency adoption) to a lengthy and uncertain period of assessment (social, medical, psychological, and financial evaluation). Once they are accepted as prospective adoptive parents, they must then undergo a lengthy, uncertain, and often undetermined waiting period, during which time they are not afforded the same opportunity as fertile couples who have nine months to prepare themselves for their new roles as parents.

If the couple adopt their child through an attorney or through an independent service ("independent" or "private" adoption), they must also undergo a period of anxiety and uncertainty as they search for a child to adopt, work with the attorney involved, present themselves in a positive manner to prospective birth parents, arrange for the financial requirements, and hope that they will finally be successful in obtaining a child.

Therapeutic Intervention

Depending on a couple's needs and preferences, they can be assisted in the pre-adoptive phase in a number of ways: (a) counseling around infertility and loss issues; (b) counseling around the decision to adopt; (c) preparation for adoption, including educational seminars, triad workshops, and special seminars; (d) participation in support groups or therapeutic groups; (e) participation in self-help groups both for the resolution of infertility, such as

RESOLVE, and for preparation for adoptive parenthood through adoptive parents groups or triad groups; and (f) reading and the use of audiovisual resource materials.

Couples preparing for adoption can be assisted by supportive, nonjudgmental exploration of painful feelings surrounding loss, uncertainty, and inadequacy. Information and education regarding grief reactions is valuable, and will assist the couple in identifying and accepting their feelings as normal reactions to their situation. Support groups can then further serve to normalize their feelings.

Issues Related to the Placement of the Child in the Adoptive Home

Infancy

The placement of a child into the adoptive home brings a new set of adjustments for the adoptive parents.

A lack of adoptive parent role models. Kirk (1984) described the fact that it is more difficult for adoptive parents to find role models for adoptive parenthood compared to non-adoptive parenthood.

The need to recognize and come to terms with issues of difference. Kirk (1984) identified two coping strategies employed by adoptive parents in their effort to overcome what they perceive to be their role handicap: (a) rejection of difference, which serves to deny feelings of loss, inadequacy, and anxiety over meeting the demands of adoptive parenthood, and (b) acknowledgment of difference, which enables the adoptive parents to openly share concerns, questions, and feelings associated with adoption. Brodzinsky (1984) has elaborated on Kirk's model to suggest that adoptive parents sometimes confuse the concept of difference with the concept of deficit, and that this is the basis for their denial. According to Brodzinsky, the consequence of denying difference is that the adoptive family will create a less open and trusting environment. Within such a family, the adopted child will be reluctant to express his or her feelings of difference, and this will foster feelings of alienation. Some families reflect a third pattern: insistence-of-difference, a more extreme coping strategy in which the family emphasizes the differences of their adoptive status and this becomes the central focus of the family's identity. In this instance, heredity can be blamed for their child's behavioral or other difficulties.

One result of the role handicap sometimes felt by adoptive parents is the belief that they do not have the right to parent — that they are not entitled to be parents. On some level, they feel that they have stolen their child from the birth parents. A compensatory adjustment to this feeling can be material and emotional overindulgence of their child, with a tendency to be overprotective.

The lack of family and community support. Extended family members may intentionally or unintentionally be unsupportive, and the larger community may be critical ("What a shame they couldn't have a child of their very own and were forced to adopt"). This may contribute to feelings of stigma or shame associated with adoption, which then lead to intense feelings of isolation. Few, if any, specific religious or cultural traditions or ceremonies exist to mark the arrival of a new family member in the adoptive family.

The need to form attachments. An important developmental task during infancy is the bonding and attachment process between parent and child. There are several hurdles to this process in adoptive parenthood. The adoptive mother does not have the opportunity to form a prenatal relationship with her child, and after the birth there is usually no opportunity to breastfeed.

Adoptive parents may genuinely fear that their child may be taken away from them during the period after placement and before finalization. This is a more realistic fear in some states and countries, where the birth parents have the right to change their minds regarding relinquishment until the time the adoption is finalized. How the adoptive parents respond to these unique stresses influences the early relationship with the child, and hence later family adjustments.

In summary, the developmental tasks of infancy for the adoptive parents are complex ones. The bonding and attachment process is complicated by the lack of mutual biology, by the long waiting period both before and after placement, and by concerns over the issue of entitlement.

Therapeutic Intervention

The goals of intervention will center on continuing issues of infertility and grief resolution, on the complications adoptive parents may face during the legal process, on the development of an identity as an adoptive parent, on dealing with their feelings about adoption, the reactions of significant others, and their sense of entitlement to the child. The process of intervention will consist of gaining an understanding of the nature of the difficulties faced by the adoptive parents during this period. A supportive therapeutic environment will help them gain confidence in themselves. The therapist will want to:

Take a thorough history of the pre-adoption experience. This should include the couple's experience with attempts to conceive; the medical and related procedures they underwent; their response to the news of their infertility; the extent to which they have been able to resolve their grief; how they arrived at the decision to adopt; the length of their waiting period; how they prepared themselves for parenthood; the nature of support they received; and finally, how all these experiences have affected their relationship as a couple and ties with others.

Provide a supportive environment. The couple should be able to fully explore their concerns and feelings, including how they view themselves, their child, and the parenting issues. Sessions which include extended family members may be useful.

Explain the special benefits of self-help group participation. This will assist the parents to feel they are not alone and that their feelings are normal, and will offer important social contact with other adoptive parents.

Issues During the Toddler and Preschool Period

A major task for adoptive parents during this stage of development is when and how to tell their child of his or her adoptive status. This task, unique to adoptive parenthood, presents adoptive parents with a double bind. On the one hand, they are encouraged to raise their child is "as if" born to them, while having to explain the fact that this is not so.

Since the early 1950s, adoption specialists have generally recommended that parents tell their child early on of his or her adoptive status. Knight (1941) advocated this "tell early" practice to relieve the parents of their fear that the child might otherwise find out from someone outside family. Schechter (1960) advocated that the child should be told sometime between the ages of 7–10 years, emphasizing that timing is important. In other words, telling is the best accomplished when the family feels good about themselves and each other. Lawton and Gross (1964) stressed that the manner of telling will determine the child's reaction to the news. Lifton (1979) believes the child should be told by age five, even if he or she has not asked questions concerning conception.

Experts have not agreed on the appropriate time to tell the child of his or her adoptive status; most agree, however, that the child should be told sometime before latency and that the manner of telling has consequences for the child's self-esteem.

Adopted children learn most about the meaning of adoption by asking their own questions of their adoptive parents and by the answers their parents give them. How free they feel to ask questions will depend almost entirely on how secure their parents are as adoptive parents. Adoptees are quick to pick up parental feelings of ambivalence about responding to questions or imparting significant information about their adoption. The problem for some adoptive parents is that the task of telling is also a reminder of the pain of their infertility and the trauma of not giving birth to their own child. In some instances, this trauma can result in the adoptive parents describing their child's birth parents and the circumstances of his or her birth in negative terms, or they may even chose not to respond at all. Small (1987) explains that.

> Not telling — or telling in a hurried and self-conscious way — communicates to the child that adoptive status is so bad that it must not be discussed. It is a short jump from that message to an understanding that children of adoption must be bad, too ... Children of adoption who recognize that their parents are uncomfortable when they raise questions about their birth families and about having been adopted will stop asking. There children will not ask questions about their adoptive status because they are afraid that they will make their parents angry, or they are afraid to talk about adoption because they think their parents may disapprove of them if they do (p. 38).

If adoptive parents are not responsive, or if the facts as they are known are either withheld or modified in some way, adoptive parents will lose the trusting relationship they want to build with their adopted child.

A valuable contribution to our understanding of the "telling" process is made by Brodzinsky and his colleagues (Brodzinsky, Pappas, Singer, & Braff, 1981; Brodzinsky, Singer, & Braff, 1984). They found that children do not begin to understand the full meaning of adoption until they are in the middle childhood years (six to nine years), even though they may have been introduced to the concept earlier. They recommend that adoptive parents should create an atmosphere in which questions about adoption can be freely explored, when necessary. "Telling" has two components: discussion about the nature of adoption in general and the provision of information about the child's birth parents with other relevant personal information. It is not until around six years of age that most adoptive children are able to discern the difference between adoption and birth. The next step in understanding occurs between ages eight and eleven, when the child, for the first time, begins to understand and appreciate the uniqueness of his or her status and some of the complexities it entails. This realization — that there were complications associated with his or her entry into the family — can be a source of confusion and uncertainty for the adoptee.

The primary task for adoptive parents is to create an atmosphere in which free discussion about adoption can happen. Adoption revelation inevitably triggers questions and concerns, and makes adoption a family issue in which each member will come to his or her own meaning, with a greater or lesser degree of ease.

Therapeutic Intervention

Adoptive parents may seek professional help during this stage of their child's development. They will often seek support and advice on how and when to tell their child about adoption. They may need further help in working through their feelings of loss as telling comes to symbolize their lack of biological tie with their adoptive child.

We suggest that the therapist first assist the parents in collecting and feeling confident about the specific information they need in order to adequately explain his or her adoption to their child. This may require extensive fact finding and meetings with the agency or attorney who handled the adoption, because incomplete information was obtained when the placement occurred. It may also require special research and assistance from search and support specialists and groups. The adoptee wants to know what happened, when, where the birth mother and father were when conception took place, where they are now, what she "did," and what they looked like?. Other questions will arise later relative to any difficulty during the birth process, the nature of the relationship between the birth mother and birth father, specific concerns or wishes expressed at the time of relinquishment, reasons for relinquishment, significant medical or genetic problems, and where they might be living at this point in time.

Help the parents as they prepare for telling their child about adoption. (In an effort to avoid their own natural fear of abandonment and rejection, adoptive parents may tend to minimize the reality of the adoption experience and its impact on their adopted child. To have been relinquished is a hard reality, but it is a reality that adopted children want to face with their parents).

Encourage the ventilation and exploration of specific concerns about the task of telling, and, if necessary, of continuing feelings of loss and entitlement. The clinician may also want to prepare parents for the task through the use of role-play and other techniques; provide supportive therapy for all family members, if necessary, during the process of telling; and recommend that the parents attend structured workshops concerning the telling process, so that they may benefit from sharing their experience with others.

Issues During the Latency Period

Issues of Primary Concern

Responding to the adoptee's concerns and questions about adoption. As noted above, the adopted child cannot adequately comprehend the meaning of adoption until approximately the age of six years. During latency, questions and concerns arise as the adoptee begins to cope with his or her adoptive status and its complications. As the child expresses concern and confusion, adoptive parents may interpret this as evidence that they have done an inadequate job in responding to their adoptive child. Care will need to be taken to determine to what degree the child's concerns and confusions are normal responses to an abstract concept with emotional ramifications, or are more indicative of difficulties for the child which require further attention.

The need to assist the adoptee and his family with "adaptive grieving." The principal task for adoptive parents during this period is to help their child through the process of what Brodzinsky (1984) calls "adaptive grieving" — a normal process of school-age adopted children, as they begin to truly understand and feel the loss of their birth parents and their origins (sometimes siblings as well). It is during latency that the adoptee begins to express confusion and concern about his or her adoptive status. As he or she begins to comprehend the complications associated with his or her adoptive status, a sense of uncertainty develops. Adoptive parents may interpret this as evidence that they have not responded adequately to the needs of their child, especially in the area of sharing information about the birth parents and the circumstances of the adoption. (The adoptee needs very specific information about the circumstances of his or her conception and birth, the relationship between the birth parents, what their current circumstances may be, and why he or she was relinquished.) Without adequate information, their sense of helplessness and anxiety is compounded. This confusion and bewilderment is a direct result of the adoptee's increased awareness that he or she was indeed relinquished and, at the same time, became a member of a new family. "Adaptive grieving" then is a normal experience (Brodzinsky, 1986) for school age adopted children. It is sometimes misunderstood by parents and teachers alike as disturbed or troublesome behavior when, in reality, it is the result of the adopted child's ability to finally comprehend the full meaning of the loss implicit in the adoption experience.

Case Study

Mr. and Mrs. Andrews, the parents of two children James (11 — adopted) and Amy (10 — not adopted) came to discuss some difficulties they were experiencing with James, around the issue of adoption. Some months previously he had become very upset about being called a "Cabbage Patch Kid" in the school yard, after he had volunteered the information that he was adopted. Since then he has made such comments as he wishes he weren't adopted, that Amy is the favored child. There have been periods when he was hard to manage because of either sullenness or rowdiness. There were no apparent problems in the school environment.

Mr. and Mrs. Andrews were unable to conceive for a long period of time, and they adopted James soon after his birth. At about the same time, Mrs. Andrews discovered that she was pregnant, and Amy was born when James was one year old.

The therapist took a developmental history from Mr. and Mrs. Andrews and sought detailed information about the resolution of their infertility; their preparation for adoption; their differing attitudes and feelings toward James and Amy; and how they had handled the issue of adoption with James.

James was seen for one session, essentially to gain an impression of his functioning, to learn about his understanding of adoption in general and his own adoption in particular.

Mr. and Mrs. Andrews attended therapy for three sessions, during which time they over came some of their fears about James and his adoption. They had been poorly prepared for adoption, and their adjustment to adoptive parenthood had been impeded by the arrival of Amy. They had told James about his adoption at age five, before he went to school, but there had been no discussion of adoption with James since then. During therapy there were discussions about the meaning and impact of adoption on all parties, at different stages. The Andrews read widely and they generally prepared themselves well to begin talking with James about his adoption and his important place in their lives. The need to assist James to develop positive feelings about adoption was stressed. Role playing and rehearsal were used in therapy.

At follow-up, Mr. and Mrs. Andrews reported that they now felt much more relaxed, that family situations were no longer so tense, and that they (including James and Amy) were talking freely about adoption. James was also more relaxed. In addition, the Andrews had sought non-identifying information about James's birth parents from the agency, and they were planning on setting up his own personal album to record his life story.

Issues of Adolescence

Adolescence is a demanding time for most people; the adolescent adoptees movement into adulthood can perhaps be more demanding. Some of the issues for the adoptive parents are:

Managing difficult behaviors. As the adolescent adoptee begins to express strong emotions and disruptive behavior, adoptive parents may feel a sense of failure and blame themselves for possessing inadequate parenting skills. The adoptee's emerging sexuality may rekindle the pain of their own infertility. They may also be fearful that their adopted daughter, for example, may be more vulnerable to an unwanted pregnancy due to the circumstances of her own birth. Adoptive parents may be tempted to blame disruptive behavior on their child's biological origins (the "bad seed" notion).

Adoptees want their parents to respond and reach out; withdrawal by their parents can add to the residual feelings of rejection felt by many adoptees.

Remaining available to the adoptee. The adoptee wants to share her or his struggle with identity issues. This can be enhanced by the acknowledgment of a shared experience of loss (Kirk, 1984). For the adoptee, it is the loss of ties with his or her biological roots; for the adoptive parents it is the loss of the child they could not conceive. This recognition of shared loss creates an important bond of mutuality and enables adoptive parents to be supportive of the adoptee's needs.

Coping with the adoptee's increasing independence. Adolescence is the period when the young person begins the process of separation from his or her family. This can be an especially painful process for adoptive parents; they may feel especially vulnerable to the loss this separation symbolizes. They may be reminded once again of the special loss they experienced in their earlier efforts to conceive a child of their own.

Therapeutic Intervention

Individual and couple counseling should be designed to assist adoptive parents of adolescent adoptees in coping with the changes taking place in their family. In addition, individual counseling for the adolescent adoptee may be particularly useful as the issues of sexuality, identity, relationships with others, and what it means to be adopted emerge in the life of the adolescent adoptee.

Special workshops on parenting may be an effective adjunct to therapy, as may separate support groups for the adolescent adoptee (Pannor & Nerlove, 1977) and for adoptive parents, with some communication between the groups. Adolescents need an opportunity to meet alone with their peers as they learn that their own thoughts and feelings are shared by others.

Case Study

Mrs. Carter is the adoptive mother of Karen (15) and Kevin (11). She and her husband, the children's adoptive father, were divorced 5 years ago. The children go to their father's home (he is now remarried) every other weekend.

Mrs. Carter has been finding it increasingly difficult to manage Karen. She is concerned that she is keeping poor company and is becoming distressed by their arguments. Mrs. Carter also suspects that Karen has been lying and been taking small amounts of money from herself and Kevin. Mrs. Carter has not checked either of these suspicions with Karen.

Mrs. Carter sought assistance alone; she invited Karen to attend, but her daughter declined. Mrs. Carter had been feeling very unsupported in her parenting of the children, and experienced considerable relief in talking about her difficulties. She was uncertain as to how much of Karen's problems had to do with the divorce, how much to adolescence and Karen's personality, how much to her own parenting, and how much to adoption. It became very clear that all these factors were important.

A number of options for therapy were evident. Mrs. Carter alone; Mrs. Carter and Karen; Mrs. Carter, Karen and Kevin and the entire family. Mrs. Carter elected to attend alone for a number of sessions because she was benefiting a lot from talking through her difficulties, clarifying issues, and discovering new ways of relating to Karen. She reported that because she felt more supported, felt less tense, and was in greater control, her relationship with Karen and Karen's behavior improved.

Mrs. Carter explored her beliefs and attitudes about adoption, about the impact adoption has on children at different developmental stages and about the experiences and needs of adopted adolescents in particular. She began to have interesting and fruitful discussions with both children about adoption, and she and Karen began to read relevant books. She was developing an understanding that Karen was grappling with identity formation and that much of Karen's turmoil, both within the family and with friends, was a result of this.

Karen joined her mother for two sessions toward the end of therapy. A number of issues were dealt with: family rules, and the responsibilities of each member; Karen's sense of belonging to the family and identity with the family; Karen's growing need to explore life and people away from the family; and Mrs. Carter's expectations of Karen.

At followup, both Mrs. Carter and Karen reported they were getting along much better and were more tolerant of each other.

Adulthood

Many of the issues which emerge in the adoptive family are the result, to a greater or lesser extent, of how the fact of adoption has been handled in the family context.

As we discuss in some detail in the next chapter, the fear of being abandoned or rejected is basic to the adoption experience and is a common fear of adoptees, no matter what their age may be. This fear can impair the adoptee's ability to enter into relationships that require commitment and call for trust between persons. Adoptees often feel that they are somehow different and that they do not belong. This feeling may be expressed during adolescence by much testing behavior and by "drifting" in adulthood.

Because of their early separation from their birth parents and a lingering fear of further abandonment, some adoptees feel an overwhelming sense of loyalty to their adoptive parents. This can make it very difficult for the adoptee to do things or make decisions to please themselves rather than their parents. This conflict of loyalties may have ramifications at any life stage; for example, the adolescent who wants to leave home, the choice of a partner or career path, and especially the adoptee's decision to search.

It is usually during the adult years that adoptees consider searching for and having a reunion with their birth parents. (We discuss the process of search and reunion in some detail in chapter 6.) The decision to embark on a search can be prompted by a major event in the adoptee's life — engagement, marriage, or birth of a child. The search, and relationships that may develop as a result of the search, often impact on the adoptive family in special ways. Adoptive parents must decide, for example, how best to be supportive of the search, how to respond when asked to be helpful in the search process, what kind of relationship they themselves wish to have with the birth parents, and how all concerned will incorporate the birth parents into the life of the extended family.

The adoptee's decision to search often poses an unexpected threat for the adoptive parents. On some level they may view this decision as a rejection and evidence of their inadequacy as parents. They may perceive the search as the first step in a long process which will end in the "loss" of their adopted son or daughter to his or her "real parents." In reality, this is an irrational fear, because adoptees are clear about the significant role of their adoptive parents in their life.

The process of search and reunion experience will, in the long run, provide many unexpected opportunities for the adoptive family to resolve issues of personal and family identity, roles and relationships.

Perhaps the most important outcome of the search and reunion process is that it can enable the entire adoptive family to "let go of denial." Small (1987) describes how adult children of adoption tend to take with them into adulthood the belief that their adoption is the basis for their problems. However, as they experience major life events (marriage, childbirth, death of a parent) the adult adoptee becomes aware of the boundaries between themselves and their families. This awareness is the first step in beginning to acknowledge the existence of his or her birth mother and family and the reality of their shared genetic heritage. Small (1987) continues:

> Adult children who search have chosen to give up the denial. They chose to give up past enabling behaviors that for them meant denial of their needs. They give up responsibility for protecting their parents from the realities of adoptive parent status. The search is the ultimate act of reality testing (p. 40).

Case Study

Mr. and Mrs. Barnes, the adoptive parents of three children, Jill (19), Jack (22), and John (24), sought therapy to deal with the difficulties around Jill wanting to search for her birth mother. Mr. and Mrs. Barnes felt that Jill was not ready for contact and they were anxious that she may be hurt as a result. They could not understand why Jill was curious and wanted to search, while their sons had never shown any interest in the fact of adoption or their birth parents.

Jill joined her parents for the second session; she had already joined a search group and was firm in her plan to search despite her parents' hesitancy. She stated that she would like for them to give her their blessing and share with interest her progress in the search. She made it very clear that she was very fond of both her parents and her brothers, for they were her family.

Searching was discussed at great length, and Mr. and Mrs. Barnes began to see that it was a normal, though difficult, process. They read literature on search and reunions and joined Jill at the search group meetings. They enjoyed and valued meeting other triad members, and some of their fears about Jill being hurt diminished.

Mr. and Mrs. Barnes returned to the attorney who had arranged Jill's adoption and obtained information which was useful to Jill in her search.

Through counseling, Mr. and Mrs. Barnes were able to address their fears, learn about the search process and the adoptee's need to search, meet other adoptive parents who had shared their concerns, and meet other adoptees and birth parents.

General Guidelines for Intervention

The central focus of all therapeutic work with adoptive parents is helping them understand and accept the fact that the adoptive family is "structured out of loss" (Small, 1987). There is strong pressure to deny this fact and assume that the adoptive family is just like any other family. Denial of difference is the basic, principal ingredient contributing to dysfunction in the adoptive family. Assisting the family therapeutically as they work through their pain, grieve for their losses, and build on their strength and effectiveness will be the most important therapeutic role in working with adoptive parents and adoptive families.

The periods of transition and developmental change we have described in this chapter are common themes in working therapeutically with adoptive families at the following stages:

1. the pre-adoptive period when they are preparing to become parents (often after a lengthy waiting period);

2. infancy, when parenting is unfamiliar, as well as a few years later when explaining their child's adoption becomes an essential parenting task;
3. adolescence, when sexuality, identity, and independence emerge as major issues; and
4. the adult years, when search and contact may become important.

Some adoptive parents will present without identifying adoption as an issue; others will become aware of how important adoption related issues are to their family functioning after they embark on a therapeutic course. It is not unusual for the adoptive parents to identify their adopted son or daughter as the presenting problem when in fact family issues are broader and more complex.

In summary, the primary therapeutic goal in working with adoptive parents is assisting them in coping with the issues of loss and "difference." The critical issue of difference is one which all adoptive parents must cope with. Understanding and accepting additional tasks and needs of adoptive family life contribute to effective adoptive parenting. Depending on the family and its unique patterns of coping and adjustment, supportive and educative therapy can be productive for the entire family.

Finally, we emphasize that the active participation of adoptive parents in support and self-help groups (both those just for parents and those which include adoptees and birth parents) can provide powerful and enabling experiences.

Chapter 6
The Adoptee

Joanne Small (1978) describes what it is like to be an adoptee:

> Adoptive families are structured out of loss ... For the child, adoption always means a loss of relationship with emotionally significant objects and a symbolic loss of roots, a sense of genetic identity, and a sense of connectedness. Becoming disconnected from one's ancestry is perhaps the loneliest experience known. It is like floating in time and space without an anchor. It means not belonging in a way that all others belong. A pervasive sense of anxiety accompanies this experience of disconnectedness (p. 36–37).

This chapter is concerned with the adoptee's development from infancy to adulthood. While all children follow the same path of development, adopted children are exposed to a unique set of tasks which tend to complicate their development. For convenience of presentation, we use the Eriksonian stages of development as they relate to adoption and as described by Brodzinsky (1987).

STAGES OF ADOPTEE DEVELOPMENT

Infancy

The primary task of infancy is the development of a basic sense of trust in the world as a place which is both dependable and predictable. The successful accomplishment of this developmental task depends on caretakers who are confident and secure.

Because preparation for adoptive parenthood is a complex process, some adoptive parents have difficulty providing a consistently nurturing environment for their adopted child.

Also, some adopted infants have a succession of caretakers if, for example, they are placed in a foster home for several weeks or even months before permanent placement. Parental insecurity and a succession of caretakers can complicate the normal adjustment of the adopted infant and cause distress for both parents and child.

Brodzinsky (1987) explains: "If the general caretaking atmosphere is characterized by warmth and low anxiety, and if the parents are secure in their parental roles and have realistic expectations concerning their child's behavior and development, they are more likely to meet the baby's needs in ways that promote a basic sense of security. On the other hand, heightened parental anxiety, or a mismatch between parental expectations and infant characteristics and behavior ... among other factors, are likely to lead to inadequate caretaking, where the baby's needs are met inconsistently and in an unsatisfying way — thereby promoting a sense of mistrust or insecurity in the infant" (p. 30).

Toddlerhood and Preschool Period

The primary tasks of the young child are to develop a sense of autonomy and initiative, achieving both self-satisfaction and approval from parents and significant others. Parents of preschoolers are sometimes ambivalent about their child's strivings for autonomy. While taking pride in their child's strivings to be more independent and achieve more of a sense of mastery, the separation between parent and child which is already beginning to occur is a cause for parental anxiety. To successfully negotiate this stage of development, the child must feel that he or she can return to the safety of parental protection.

The preschooler's striving for autonomy and initiative may be more difficult for the adoptive family than the non-adoptive family, because it is during this period of development that parents begin to explain to their adopted child that he or she is adopted. The task of telling (explaining the adoption) is especially difficult because it confirms the biological separation between adoptive parents and their adopted child. It creates a sense of difference where none previously existed (Brodzinsky, 1987).

The adoptee's understanding of adoption and his or her feelings about being adopted will be influenced by when, what, and how he or she is told about the adoption.

School Age Years

The primary developmental themes of the school age years are the need to master things, to be industrious, and to understand. Children at this developmental stage seek challenges and satisfaction for their efforts. They especially want to be recognized and acknowledged by parents and teachers.

The Adoptee

The school age years present a special challenge for the adoptee and his parents (Brodzinsky, 1987). Although most preschool children are able to tell you that they are adopted, they do not really understand what that means until they reach the school age years. At the age of six, the adoptee begins to distinguish between birth and adoption as two disparate ways in which to enter a family (Brodzinsky, 1987). Between the ages of eight to eleven, this understanding broadens dramatically, and the adoptee comes to realize that adoption means being both chosen *and* having been given up.

As Brodzinsky (1987) further explains:

> Adopted children now begin to appreciate the uniqueness of their family status, including some of the complications it entails. For example, to be adopted means not only that one has been "chosen", but also that one has been relinquished or "given up." ... children often begin to fantasize about the circumstances surrounding relinquishment ... they not only consider the basis for their relinquishment ... the school age child ... begins to see possible solutions to the problems that once confronted the birth parents ... sometimes this leads to feelings of anger and resentment toward the birth parents; sometimes it leads to concern that the birth parents' circumstances might have changed and that they are now considering reclaiming the child (p. 35).

As the child's understanding of his or her adoptive status broadens, so does his or her confusion. Brodzinsky (1987) further explains that the school age adoptee's reactions are a normal part of the process of adaptive grieving:

> as they mature intellectually ... children come to understand the many complications associated with their family status that their parents have either ignored or downplayed in family conversations ... children's confusion during this period most often is a normal part of coping with adoption — it reflects an increasing awareness of what it means to be adopted; and it represents the beginning of a normal process of adaptive grieving ... the behavior of school-age children that is labelled by parents, teachers, and others as upsetting, troublesome, difficult, or disturbed very often is simply a reflection of the normal process of adaptive grieving ... (p. 36)."

One very common approach to the task of telling has been the use of the "chosen baby" story. The "chosen baby" story was encouraged by many agencies when it was felt that the actual circumstances of the birth and relinquishment should not be revealed. Many adoptees were told this story and little more with the result that, in the absence of other information, they expanded this concept to include fantasies that they were saved from bad or incompetent birth parents, that they must be grateful to their adoptive parents for having been saved, and that they must please their adoptive parents in order to be grateful.

Case study
David is an 11-year old adopted boy who was referred for behavioral

problems at school. During the intake interview, his parents reported that David was not keeping up with his homework, was disruptive in class, and was picking fights with several other students. They also indicated that David appeared more restless and irritable than usual and that he seemed withdrawn at times. His parents both agreed that David's behavioral changes began several months earlier and that, coincidentally, questions about his adoption had also increased.

A history indicated that David was adopted at birth through a local private agency. David's parents had tried to have a child of their own for four years but were unable to conceive. No medical complications were found and, rather than continue their fruitless efforts, they decided to adopt. They described David as a "good baby" who seemed happy and well adjusted. He cried little and was able to form attachments to them easily. By age five, he began to ask questions about how babies are made. His parents had been advised by the agency to tell David about his adoptive status when he showed an interest in babies. They were also advised to emphasize that he was wanted and chosen.

When David asked his parents how babies came into this world, they told him there were two ways, one by birth and one by adoption. They explained to David that he was adopted. They told him how much his Mom and Dad wanted a child but couldn't have one, how they fell in love with him the moment they saw him and that, of all the babies at the adoption agency, he was the most special one. They explained that another woman gave birth to David but that she was unable to provide him with a good home so she made sure he got what he needed. David seemed to take all this information in stride and even appeared to feel special for some time. He told his school mates with pride that he was adopted.

Over the years, David continued to ask questions about adoption. He especially wanted to know about his other parents, who they were, and why he was given up. His adoptive parents had difficulty answering his questions since they had little specific information themselves.

Just prior to bringing David to therapy, David's mother discovered that she was pregnant. It appeared to David's parents that shortly after he was told about the pregnancy, his questions about adoption increased and his school problems began.

The therapist talked with David's parents about the stages of adoptee development and adaptive grieving, and let them know that his fear of being displaced was heightened by a new baby along the way. The therapist indicated that the lack of background information about David's adoption was further contributing to his behavioral problems.

David's parents, with this newfound understanding, were eager to help him. They returned to the adoption agency to increase and update their knowledge of David's background so that they could share it with him. They constructed a "Life Story" book that included photos and text for David to have (Connor, et al., 1985; Backhaus, 1984). They joined an adoptive parent support group to better understand the impact of adoption in their lives, and they offered David the chance to join a group of adoptees his age.

The family was now able to talk freely about adoption and David's behavior and mood slowly improved.

Adolescence

According to Erikson (1963, 1968), the primary theme of the adolescent period is a search for answers to the question: "Who am I?"

Dramatic changes in physical appearance and moods associated with hormonal changes create a feeling of being out of control. To maintain a sense of control and continuity through time, adolescents attempt to link their current sense of self with past perceptions of self.

Midford (1987) describes the importance of identity issues in the adoptee's experience:

> Identity is of particular relevance to adoptees. By virtue of the process of adoption they leave their genealogical identity behind a legal curtain upon placement with their adoptive parents. A mystery exists because the individual adoptee's identity is based on incomplete and often unobtainable information. Research has shown identity to be a major component in understanding a number of aspects of adoptee's lives, particularly as it relates to genealogical issues. (p. 1)

The adolescent adoptee is handicapped in his or her quest for a sense of a common bond and by a lack of genealogical knowledge and thus has difficulty linking past with present. The question: "Who am I?" can become: "Who could I have been?" The ensuing feelings of confusion and uncertainty are partly an extension of the process of adaptive grieving, but it is more complex: in latency the adoptee grieved for the loss of his or her birth parents, but in adolescence, the adoptee grieves for a lost part of the self. (Brodzinsky, 1987).

Brodzinsky (1987) observed coping patterns used by adoptees to resolve adoption-related issues. He noted that some adolescents can confront adoption openly and find a way to integrate this reality into their self-concept. Others attempt to define the meaning of adoption but cannot reach a conclusion. Still others avoid the issue and deny or suppress their feelings.

It is not uncommon for the adoptee to assume one of two roles in the family — that of the "good adoptee" or that of the "bad adoptee" (Lifton, 1979). The "good adoptee" conforms to parental expectations and is outwardly content and agreeable. The "bad adoptee" rebels against parental authority and expectations. The "good adoptee" appears to conform as a defense against a deeply felt fear of further abandonment, while the "bad adoptee" is motivated by the need to act out the feeling that he or she must have been "no good" to have been given away.

Adulthood

The primary psychosocial task of adulthood is developing a capacity for intimacy. Adulthood is a period in which there is a further consolidation of one's identity through such important life events as marriage, the creation of a family, and career development.

Adult adoptees sometimes take emotional "baggage" with them into adulthood: feelings of isolation, alienation, difficulties with making comitments in relationships, low self-esteem, lack of ability to trust others, and anger.

Denial

We emphasize again the significant role of denial in the structure and functioning of the adoptive family and its impact on the adoptee. Small (1987) describes the fact that adoptees may assume one or a combination of roles as part of this adjustment pattern: the enabler, the family hero, the scapegoat, or the lost child. The enabler (just as in the alcoholic family) supports the myth that the adoptive family is just like the nonadoptive family; the family hero (often an overachiever) behaves in such a way as to make the adoptive family proud of him or her; adoptees who become scapegoats act out their anger and hostility; and the lost adoptee withdraws, avoids risking failure, and avoids intimate contact with the adoptive family.

Small (1987) continues her analysis by outlining three stages of adult development which describe the process of letting go of denial and moving on to a realistic appraisal of oneself:

Stage one: an emerging awareness and enlightenment. The adoptee begins to understand how the need to know is a matter of some urgency and part of his or her birthright.

Stage two: giving up past enabling behaviors. The adoptee stops trying to protect the adoptive parents from the realities of adoption, maintaining "loyalty" to their adoptive parents at the expense of her or his own needs, allowing others to be in "control" of their destiny. The adoptee begins to "address some of the core issues and feelings that relate to their adoptive status" (Small, 1987 p. 40) and begin the process of searching.

The search is the ultimate act of reality testing. By searching, the adult children of adoption begin to gain a sense of accomplishment. By engaging in a search, they can achieve a sense of control over their adoption and over what has happened to them as a result of it. Search means getting in touch with painful feelings of anger and loss that have been long denied. In stage two, adult children begin to trust their true feelings and recognize their own experiences as being valid. (Small, 1987, p. 40).

Stage three: integration. The adult adoptee finally comes to terms with the reality of his ancestry and the unique place it holds in his or her life. Lifelong questions are answered and reality replaces fantasy. There is a sense of completeness, of roots, for the first time in one's life. Thoughts and feelings are not as separated as they once were and there is a sense of new-found peace and satisfaction.

The fear of being abandoned or rejected is common among adoptees of all ages. For some adult adoptees, this fear results in a reluctance to trust and make lasting commitments. For others, they find themselves repeating a pattern of either setting themselves up to be rejected or of rejection before they, themselves, are rejected.

Many adoptees have feelings of frustration, hopelessness, and impotence about themselves and in relation to the rest of the world. They feel that their adoption experience is beyond their control, that their life has been "masterminded," and that there is little they can do to create their own direction and exercise their own potency.

Adoptees often feel they are different and that they do not belong. This feeling of not belonging can be reflected in "drifting" in adulthood.

Many adult adoptees acknowledge an overwhelming sense of loyalty to their adoptive parents which makes it difficult for them to take responsibility for their own lives. Instead, important life decisions are too often made on the basis of what would be pleasing to their adoptive parents rather than to themselves. For example, the need to chose a partner or decide upon a career path can present a crisis over conflicting loyalties between self and adoptive parents.

SEARCH AND REUNION

The decision to search

Adult adoptees report they rarely meet or get to know other adoptees as they are growing up. As they read about others who have searched (see Suggested Readings) or join a search and support group, they begin to realize that they have minimized or denied the significance of adoption in their lives. Joining a search and support group thus becomes a "coming out" experience.

As adoptees begin to acknowledge to themselves and others that they are adopted, they also begin to realize how important it would be if they reconstructed the past and perhaps even met with their birth parents. They realize, at about the same time, that there is much information they do not have: their name at birth (before their adoption record was sealed), the religious and ethnic background of their birth parents, their health history, why they were "given up," and the kind of relationship which existed between their birth mother and birth father. They realize that they do not even know if they are genetically vulnerable to alcoholism, heart disease, cancer, or even more serious genetically transmitted conditions.

Adoptees fear marrying a blood relative, and they wonder if they will someday pass their birth mother or birth father on the street. Many adoptees wonder if (and secretly hope that) they will unexpectedly "run into" missing family members, and they deliberately look for people who resemble themselves. Adoptees can be cautious. In dating, and later in seeking a marriage partner, they want to be sure they will be accepted in their status as adoptees before making a commitment to marriage or other relationships. Often adoptees will withhold the fact that they are adopted if they sense or fear that they will not be accepted.

Most adoptees prefer to initiate their search on their own. They are reluctant to ask their adoptive parents for information or other kinds of assistance, partly out of concern that they will be regarded as disloyal, but also because they want to begin taking control over a part of their lives that has never been within their control.

In retrospect, adoptees report that the decision to search is, in a very significant way, an effort to overcome their sense of existential alienation and loneliness.

As we described in chapter 5, the decision to search is fundamentally a decision to begin letting go of denial (Small, 1987).

The decision to search is often triggered by significant life events such as marriage, pregnancy and childbirth, medical problems, or the death of a parent. It may also be triggered by a sense of unfinished business and loss as one grows older.

Life events which may lead to the decision to search include, but are not limited to, the following:

1. The decision to start a family which can contribute to the need to know what, if any, unknown potential genetic defects may be lurking in one's background.

2. Engagement and marriage can stimulate a desire to reconnect and to forge a link between an unknown part of oneself as one faces an unpredictable future.

3. For an adopted woman, pregnancy and childbirth can create a powerful longing for contact with the birth mother (and father). The experience of childbirth for both the male and female adoptee can contribute to a deep appreciation for an identification with the intense pain of childbirth and relinquishment.

4. The death of an adoptive parent and the accompanying feelings of loss may create an unusually strong void for the adult adoptee; it may also free the adoptee from a reluctance to begin a search.

5. Periods of distress and transition such as marital separation, divorce, or death in the family often serve to increase awareness of one's own vulnerability and stimulate the need to know about one's genealogical heritage.

The process of the search

Although few statistics are available (Hoksbergen, 1986); we know from experience and from informal reports that search and reunion has become a widespread activity in the last 15 years in the United States, Canada, Britain, Australia, and many European countries. Hardly a day passes in which there is not some reference in the media to an adoptee–birth parent search and reunion. Search groups can now be found in most major cities and handbooks (Rillera, 1981) are now available which provide specific information on the step-by-step process of the search.

The search process can be a difficult one in terms of time, financial expense, and emotional energy. It is not unusual for a search (either one initiated by the adoptee or by the birth parent) to take at least three years or more. Because the original birth records are sealed, most adoptees (and birth parents) begin their search without knowing their name at birth. They must rely, therefore, on public documents, court records (these are seldom released even for urgent medical need), non-identifying information from the agency or the attorney who handled the adoption, the recollections of those familiar with what took place, and registration in a reunion registry (such as the International Soundex Reunion Registry in Carson City, Nevada). The latter has increasingly resulted in matches between birth parents and adoptees.

Because the search is such a laborious and frustrating experience, adoptees (and birth parents) are greatly aided and supported if they participate in search and support groups. These groups provide both hands-on technical assistance in searching and invaluable emotional support.

Many of these groups strongly advocate legislative reform and believe that it is the adoptee's constitutional right to have full access to his or her birth record, on demand, at age 18 or 21. This "right to know" movement seeks reform of legislation which mandated the sealed record practice many years ago.

The primary objective of the adoptee search is to locate the birth mother. Search and reunion with the birth mother then leads to the decision to find the birth father. This is not always the case, of course, but generally the first contact is with the birth mother. She is often the only source of reliable information about the identity and whereabouts of the birth father.

The first procedural step in the search process is to find the name of the birth parent.

Stages of the search

The search process usually follows a pattern of distinctive stages. These stages of the search have been eloquently described by Betty Jean Lifton (1979) and we draw on her work.

The initial stage, *crossing the threshold*, often takes place only after a lengthy period of hesitation and ambivalence about whether or not to search. This period of slow preparation can be triggered, as we noted above, by a significant event in one's life. It is an important step in the process.

In the second stage, *obsession*, the search becomes an all-consuming activity. It is a remarkable phase, for once the decision to search is made, it becomes a driving force in one's life. Hours are spent examining records, researching leads; it is like working on a major mystery. This stage is complete when the birth parent has been located — i.e., their whereabouts and identity are discovered.

The third stage, *limbo*, is almost like a "cooling off" period; it is a time of consolidation of thoughts and feelings as the reality of the birth parent(s) is integrated into one's sense of self and the world. Feelings of ambivalence are strongly felt: "How can I take the final step and call my birth mother?" "I'm afraid she will reject me again." "What if she is married and hasn't told her husband about me?" "What if I call and find she is dead?"

In the final stage, *penetration of the veil*, contact is finally made, either by phone, letter, or personal visit.

The reunion

The reunion between adoptee and birth parent is an extraordinary experience. (Betty Jean Lifton, 1979 describes the experience in more detail than we will do so here.) At the heart of the experience is the opportunity, finally, to feel grounded and whole, in spite of whether or not expectations are met. It is tempting to say that the process is just as important as what you find. In some sense that is true; however, the process of "finding," of coming to the end of a long quest, is part of the entire experience, because the person you find occupies such a unique place in the life of the adoptee. The reunion can be a time of healing and reconcilliation. It is not a panacea for life's ills; however, it is an experience that generally leads to personal growth and positive mental health.

There is no set pattern of post-reunion relationships. In some cases, birth parent(s) and adoptee incorporate each other into the life of their extended family; in others, contact becomes infrequent. All adoptees want to know and hear firsthand why they were conceived and why they were given up. These questions can be very threatening for the birth parent(s); many withdraw on first contact, only to reach out very soon thereafter. Adoptive parents must decide how they will incorporate the birth parent(s) into their lives. Some families turn to religious ceremonies; others reject the birth parent(s) out of a sense of fear and competition for the loyalty of their adoptee.

Case example

Anne is a 23-year-old student who initially came to therapy for difficulties she was having in her relationship with her boyfriend. She explained that she wanted to explore her feelings and options. She complained of feeling anxious, confused, and mildly depressed. She indicated that although there were no major difficulties in her three-year-old relationship with her boyfriend, she felt restless and ready to move on. After some discussion, it became clear that Anne's boyfriend wanted to marry and start a family, while she wanted to finish college and begin her career.

In the early stages of therapy, Anne mentioned that she was adopted and that she had fleeting thoughts about searching for her birth mother. She had two concerns, however: that she would hurt her adoptive parents if she began a search, and that it would be too hard to do since she didn't even have her mother's name. Yet thoughts of searching were much on her mind and had become even more frequent recently.

Anne's therapist explored her feelings about adoption in some detail and suggested that she read some materials and join a local search and support group, which she did. She was quite excited about her experience in the group, having never talked intimately with other adoptees. Most compelling for her was the experience of meeting several birth mothers and hearing about the pain of their relinquishment and how much they cared about the child they relinquished.

Anne explained in therapy that when she had asked questions about her adoption as a child, her parents were initially responsive but then became impatient when she asked more questions as an adolescent. She felt that her questions posed some threat to her parents, and this kept her from asking the questions most on her mind.

As time passed, Anne felt more strongly about searching and decided she would begin the process. Anne and her therapist role-played how she would approach her parents and adoption agency for the information she needed. To her surprise, her parents were quite responsive and provided her with the amended birth certificate and a copy of the final adoption decree. Anne also continued to attend her search and support group and found willing members to guide her in the search process.

Anne worked on her search with great energy, spending several hours a week on the phone or at the library examining records. She described her emotions as "like being on a roller coaster" — she was depressed when a potential lead did not materialize and became elated when she realized some success in the search process.

During one of the subsequent sessions, Anne's therapist suggested she explore her feelings and fantasies about her birth mother. What did she hope to find? What if her birth mother didn't want to meet her?

After several weeks, Anne called to share the fact that she had located her birth mother. When she came for therapy, she was excited but then explained that she was fearful of taking the next step — personal contact. "What if she won't talk to me or even acknowledge I exist?" She and her therapist used guided imagery to work through some of these conflicting feelings.

At a subsequent session, Anne reported that she had talked with her birth mother over the phone and it had been a "peak experience." She had decided to call, picked up the phone several times, and then hung up. She finally found the courage to call. She described the four-hour phone conversation in some detail, and how she and her birth mother had agreed to meet in two weeks. In the meantime, they promised to share letters and photos.

As the time for the reunion approached, Anne worked with the therapist in preparing a list of questions to ask her birth mother.

After reunion, Anne spent a long session talking about her meeting with her birth mother and reliving that experience of crying, laughing, hugging, and staring at each other.

For several months following the reunion, Anne and her birth mother continued to write and talk on the phone, with occasional visits. As time passed their relationship seemed to become less intense and more like other relationships. She met her birth parents' other children and enjoyed having a half-brother and half-sister. After several more months, Anne finally got up the courage to ask about her birth father and found that he had died several years after her birth.

Therapy concluded at this point with Anne sharing how much more at peace she felt with herself. She described the fact that she just felt more settled in her life, more grounded and more in control. As therapy ended, Anne decided to stay in her relationship with her boyfriend, since he had agreed to wait until she finished her education.

THERAPEUTIC CONSIDERATIONS — IMPLICATIONS FOR INTERVENTION

Several common themes dominate the adoptee's experience and suggest appropriate interventions.

First, the fear of abandonment and related concerns about self-worth and vulnerability are commonly experienced. Adoptees also tend to be unusually sensitive to experiences they perceive as holding the potential for rejection.

Second, denial is employed by the adoptee and his or her family (see chapter 5) and this can become the basis for substantial dysfunction. Small (1987) explains that

> the child's basic sense of self develops around a faulty belief system. It is based on denial that there is any difference between being born to one's parents and being adopted. When this situation occurs, all of the family members unwittingly become codependents to a denial process. This process is analagous to codependence that occurs in alcoholic families ... a dysfunctional pattern of living and problem solving that is grounded in denial. Within the family system, this pattern of denial is nurtured by a set of unwritten and unspoken rules (p. 36) ...
> To understand why this is so, we should look at some of the characteristics common to both adoptive and codependent families:
> * The family structures itself around a problem. in an adoptive family the child's past is considered a deficit the family should try to overcome.
> * The family tries to hide the problem. The adoptive family attempts to structure itself as if it were a nonadoptive family.
> * Adoptive family members have difficulty identifying and expressing feelings about adoption.
> * Communications related to adoption is faulty. They are often confusing, inconsistent, and emotional, and reflect a denial of reality.
> * Fantasy replaces reality.
> * Attitudes and behaviors related to adoption tend to become rigid.
> * There are feelings of powerlessness over one's life, as in feeling a loss of control over what has happened and not really having had a chance.
> * Members of the family feel responsible for the behavior or feelings of others; they feel like they have to make up for something that is missing.
> * Members of the family share a basic sense of shame or low self-esteem.
> * Family members show a strong need for approval from others in both the family and social system (p. 36).

The problem with denial can also present a special issue for helping professionals if they, too, fall into a codependent relationship with their clients, becoming, "professional enablers," and engaging in "the same kind of behaviors — avoidance, protection, covering up, and denial — with which the adoptive family deny their difference" (Small, p. 41).

The goals of intervention are (a) to affirm the validity of the adoptee's perceptions of his or her adoption experience and assist in the process of self-realization and integration of past and present; and (b) to assist the adoptee in clarifying feelings (e.g., anger, hurt, fear) and understanding the basis for those feelings as they may or may not be rooted in the adoption experience.

Just as with birth parents, helping professionals need to work patiently with adoptees as they tell and retell their story. This is a key part of the therapeutic process and serves to enable the adoptee to gain perspective and realize control.

The essential elements of the adoptee's "story" are reflected in the following questions:

When were you told about your adoption?
What were you told?
How were you told?
Who told you?
How was it explained to you?
What questions did you have that you were too afraid to ask?
How did you feel when you were told you were adopted?
What was your understanding of the meaning of your adopted status in your family?
What would you like to know about your birth parents and why they relinquished you?
What fantasies and feelings do you have about them now?
Who have you told about your adopted status and how did they react?
If the search and reunion has taken place:
    How has the search and reunion affected your life?
    Did you find what you were looking for?

The value of adoptee self-help groups

These groups are especially helpful for the adoptee both as an adjunct to therapy and as part of the continuing process of self exploration and understanding.

They help overcome feelings of isolation and provide invaluable insight into the experience of all triad members; they assist members in validating and normalizing their experience and reduce the sense of difference; they offer specific assistance in search and reunion techniques, useful at any stage in the process; and they provide an environment in which feelings can be explored without injury.

In conclusion, helping professionals, clinicians, facilitators of self-help groups, and specialized adoption workers can all make a significant contribution to the quality of life and to the healthy development of individuals affected by the adoption experience.

This contribution can be made by viewing adoption as a life course experience for all members of the triad and their extended families, rather than an event that takes place at a single point in time, by assisting triad members as they seek to empower themselves and come to terms with the experience of loss so central to the adoption experience, and, lastly, by working collaboratively with affiliated professionals and community leaders to help promote public understanding of adoption as a life course experience.

Chapter 7
Special Issues in Adoption

In this chapter we discuss aspects of current adoption practice that are different from traditional adoption practice. The clinical implications of these practices may become the concern of the post-adoption practitioner. These practices include *special needs adoption, semi-open* and *open adoption, transracial adoption* (including inter-country adoption), *surrogacy,* and *artificial insemination by donor (AID).* While many of the clinical issues of these practices will be similar to those arising from traditional adoption practice, some issues will be more specific to a particular procedure.

SPECIAL NEEDS ADOPTION

"Special needs adoption" refers to the adoption of children who have (a) experienced early trauma (abuse and neglect); (b) experienced multiple placements before a decision for permanency (adoption) has been made ("systems children"); and (c) developmental disabilities or intellectual or physical impairment.

Until ten to fifteen years ago, such children were never considered for adoption. Since then, enormous efforts have been made to recruit families to care for those children who have special needs. The philosophy that all children have the right to grow up in the context of permanent family membership has brought about what we refer to as "permanency planning."

Adoptive families have been selected primarily on the basis of their ability to meet the needs of a particular child. In special needs adoption, adoption practice has become more truly child-centered. Such adoptive families are likely to be very special families, with atypical strengths and resources.

All children go into adoptive families with a genealogical heritage, early life experiences (including birth), and a bond to their family of origin. The earlier life experiences and the bond with the child's family of origin will bear a more significant influence on the adjustment of the special needs child, both pre- and post-placement. The interaction with these factors (e.g., personality, developmental stage) plays a significant role.

Adoptive parents of special needs children will seek services for many reasons at different stages. They will be seeking both support and therapeutic services from the self-help sector and also from the professional sector. Adoption agencies involved in the placement of special needs children tend to provide the adoptive families with ongoing support and services, given the extent and nature of the children's problems prior to placement.

Adoptive parents typically seek services because of difficulties with the extreme behaviors of their adopted child(ren); such behaviors can be the result of the child's earlier life experiences, factors associated with the adoption, or an interaction of both. Among the earlier life experiences that may present problems are physical, emotional, sexual abuse; neglect; lack of a significant attachment experience; and failure to mourn significant losses (Jewett, C. L., 1982).

In addition, children who suffer developmental disabilities or physical or intellectual impairment may also have had periods of institutional care. A significant proportion of special needs children come from racial minority groups. Where possible, these children are now being placed in adoptive homes with similar racial and ethnic backgrounds.

Increasingly, adoptive parents are seeking services that will enhance and support their role. Such services can have a more preventive function for all members of the adoptive family.

After a long period of struggling to make the placement work, some adoptive families feel that either they, other family members, or the adopted child do not have the resources to proceed. The dilemma for all, including the practitioner, is determining to what extent support and services will enable this family to restore its functioning to a healthy level. If such restoration is not possible, then all parties need to be prepared and assisted with the process of terminating the adoptive placement. The issue of disruption is a very difficult one, and will be discussed further under interventions.

Clinical Issues

The therapist must be attentive to the child's pre-adoptive history and determine how and to what extent earlier life experiences are contributing to the presenting problems.

Common behavior problem for special needs children include acute lying and stealing, underachievement in school, and difficulties in forming and maintaining friendships (e.g., loneliness, fighting, many superficial friendships). Melina (1986) considers these problems to be the result of: (a) lack of conscience (the child is unable to differentiate between right and wrong, and is unable to demonstrate remorse or regret when she or he has done something wrong; (b) an inability to differentiate and express feelings; and (c) an inability to form attachments; to respond to demonstrations of love and caring.

The special needs child may be very angry and full of rage about the trauma and circumstances of his or her earlier life experiences. These strong feelings are usually expressed in an indirect manner, causing further emotional difficulties for the child and tension in family relationships.

The special needs child may have unhappy memories and associations with various professionals (e.g., police, physicians, social workers) and may be angry with and fearful of subsequent contact with professionals.

Not all special needs children will automatically be able to handle the demands of forming new and permanent attachments. Their receptiveness may be enhanced by assisting them in mourning past relationships, and by helping them place their pasts in the context of the present and future. However, it is important to remember that the child needs to attach to the adoptive parents, not the therapist.

When the adoptive family presents with serious difficulties, it is important *not* to assume that they are looking to have their child removed. The issue of commitment, however, is one that needs to be explored openly and honestly from the perspective of the adoptive parents, the child, and other family members. It may be beneficial for the family to make the commitment all over again.

Family counseling approaches should be avoided until it is clear that the child is ready emotionally and socially to become part of this new family.

Support the adoptive parents in their role and in their attempts to build a nurturing family environment. Recognize that it is their resources and strengths that make it possible for them to care for a special needs child.

Adoption will have an impact on the total family functioning and the functioning of individual members; thus, the family needs to be an integral part of any intervention plan.

The adoptive parents must understand the child's limitations and strengths and modify their expectations accordingly. Periodic reviews of the child's progress, ideally by a third party, will provide useful feedback for all concerned. Expectations can then be further modified.

Many special needs adoptive families feel that they are not understood by their family and friends. This heightens their need for support. They also have a need to seek the friendship and support of families with similar experience. The self-help groups formed by special needs adoptive families are among the stronger and more active groups in the post-adoption area.

Interventions

Much of the post adoption intervention in special needs adoption has its roots in the pre-placement phase, with the preparation of both the child and the family for placement. The importance of this preparatory work cannot be overstated. However, sometimes the specific issues are not apparent, or problems do not arise until the placement is made. Many of the interventions which will be described below are appropriate whenever the need is apparent.

Helping the child deal with the past

Life Story book: Bourgnignon and Watson (1987) and Melina (1986) both discuss the importance and use of a life story book. It is essentially a means of documenting in sequence the people, places, and events in the child's past. The process of developing the book can become a therapeutic tool which helps the child put his or her past into perspective (Backhaus, 1984; Connor, et al., 1985).

Grief Work: The child who has suffered the loss of important attachments will need to mourn those losses. Sad, angry, and hurt feelings need to be expressed and validated. He or she will also need to discuss the meaning of the loss, at a level appropriate to her or his stage of emotional and cognitive development. Jewett (1982) describes grief work with children.

Graphic Techniques: The famograph and the genogram (described in chapter 3) are techniques which can be used with children, to help them understand their past and to find a way of integrating it with their new family circumstances. However, the use of these techniques will depend on the child's level of understanding.

Family Sessions: The family context is an appropriate one for having the child consider which aspects of his or her past life he or she wishes to incorporate into their new life situation, and how this can be done (e.g., certain family traditions or celebrations).

Group Therapy: The group therapy format is appropriate, since it allows many of the child's maladaptive interaction patterns and behaviors to be dealt with in a supportive environment. The child also realizes that there are others who have difficulties similar to her or his own.

Maintenance and development of current placement

Attachment Work: The child can be encouraged to develop new healthy relationships with the adoptive parents in a variety of ways. Cline and

Anderson, in Grabe (1986) *describe procedures that primarily involve the use of physical contact (holding) until the child can trust his or her parents and relinquish the need for control. Melina (1986) discusses the use of touch, especially with children who have been abused in the past. Bourgnignon and Watson (1987) state that attachment work is important at three levels: it promotes acceptance and feelings of security between those living together, it encourages family members to know each other better and enjoy an independent relationship, and it promotes a genuine attachment between child and parents.*

Parent Training Workshops: These educate and train the adoptive parents in various areas of parenting, including managing difficult behaviors. They also afford parents important support.

Family Counseling: Once a child's position in the family has been established, family sessions are useful to help the family develop a sense of a future together, discuss any problematic issues or adjustments to be made; and decide on family rules and rituals, to be observed by family members.

Crisis Intervention: The ability to respond to a crisis arising within the adoptive family because of the behavior or needs of the child can be useful, and may ultimately prevent a breakdown in the placement. Programs offering immediate assistance and suggestions for long-term solutions will be valued. Sessions with the adoptee for the purpose of supporting the parents will assist the parents with management of difficult behaviors. They may also help to clarify the family's expectations in light of progress, and provide feedback; sessions with the adoptive parents, as the need arises, are useful. The use of video recordings document the progress and provide feedback.

Support Groups: Self-help groups, either for adoptive parents or for parents and others concerned with special issues (e.g., cerebral palsy) offer invaluable support. Agency-facilitated support groups, available in some locations, are often valued by the participants.

Residential Treatment: Out-of-home care may be an important means of providing the child with intensive therapy and relief for all parties.

Respite Care: It is appropriate for many adoptive parents to enjoy a break from their special needs child. This may be on a regular basis or only as the need arises. It is important to encourage adoptive parents to nurture themselves.

Subsidy: In some states and countries, subsidies are available to adoptive parents of special needs children when the child has pre-existing conditions. These subsidies are an important part of the adoption service and are used to purchase services (e.g., therapy, tutoring, respite care).

Disruption
Despite the best intentions and efforts of those concerned, some special needs adoption placements do not work. Bourgnignon and Watson (1987) state this can be due to one of three reasons: (a) the child lacks the capacity to integrate into the adoptive family; (b) the placement was a mismatch in terms of needs and resources; or (c) either the child, the parents, or both were not ready for the placement to proceed.

If a decision is reached to terminate the placement, it must be done in such a way that the dignity and integrity of all concerned are maintained. Counseling will enable the child, the adoptive parents, and family members to gain insight into the precipitating factors, value mementos and memories of their lives together, and say goodbye. Both relief and grief are likely responses.

Finally, it is apparent that the overall success of special needs adoption as a practice depends partly on the quality of the placement work, the pre-adoption preparatory work, and the post-adoption support services available to and utilized by the adoptive families.

OPEN ADOPTION

Open adoption refers to an adoption with open channels of communication between adoptive parents and birth parents. It includes the exchange of identifying or non-identifying information as well as face-to-face contact. This exchange may be on an irregular or ongoing basis.

In open adoption, agreements relative to the nature and frequency of communication and contact are negotiated between birth parents and adoptive parents; these agreements may be recorded in written form although they are not legally enforceable. The legal rights of birth parents are no different than those in traditional adoption, despite the belief that they may have had their rights increased. Open adoption is an attempt to acknowledge the wishes and needs of birth parents more fully.

Open adoption arrangements may involve the adoption agency as the third party; the agency will thus take the role of negotiator and mediator with regard to ongoing contact, receiving and dispensing information and dealing with any conflicts that arise.

Ideally, open adoption arrangements are based on the needs of the parties to the adoption at the time of adoption. Their wishes and desires are reflected in the decisions made.

Those advocating open adoption emphasize the benefit derived from the fact that all parties know each other rather than having little or no firsthand knowledge.

Clinical Issues

The quality of preparation for an open adoption prior to the formulation of the adoption placement will enhance the adjustment of all parties and will mitigate against future difficulty.

The interests of birth parents and adoptive parents need to be represented fairly; the use of separate advocates concerned with the welfare and interests of each party is strongly suggested.

For all parties, there is a need to carefully assess the ongoing implications of openness (e.g., the responsibilities involved and the unexpected difficulties).

The lack of longitudinal studies regarding outcomes of open adoption make it difficult for birth parents and adoptive parents to make informed decisions regarding such an arrangement.

The ability of all the parties to cope with the demands of open adoption and its long term practicalities will be important elements in the assessment process, both in the pre-adoption period and in the ongoing evaluation of contact after the adoption has been finalized.

Because open adoption may prevent birth parents from adequately dealing with the pain and loss of relinquishment (grief work), they may require special assistance in putting their adoption experience into perspective. Open adoption may also threaten the adoptive parent's sense of security (a threat they may not be aware of during the early months of the child's life), and this may impair the necessary attachment process between adoptive parents and their adopted child.

All concerned need to be aware of the lack of community support for open adoption; as they enter into open adoption, even members of their extended families may be critical and unsupportive.

A positive benefit to adoptive parents of open adoption is their first hand knowledge of the birth parents. They can talk with their adopted child from actual experience; such an arrangement leaves no room for fantasies, myths, and third party interpretations of the birth parents. For the adoptee, open adoption means that he or she is able to ask for and receive more complete information about his or her origins at each stage of development, as compared to "closed adoption." In addition, it would appear that for the adoptee, issues of abandonment and rejection are not as severe as those experienced with more closed adoption arrangements.

Secrecy is greatly reduced as an issue for all concerned, and issues of trust and betrayal can be minimized.

Adoptive parents must cope more actively with the issue of where to draw family boundaries; birth parents must deal with the same issue, but not from a parenting perspective. And all parties must be willing to renegotiate their relationship as the adoptee's needs change during his or her growth and development.

For the adoptee, open adoption should enhance identity formation in later years; however, it may contribute to a confused sense of belonging if firm family boundaries are not drawn or if there is some role confusion.

The adoptee may have difficulty integrating the knowledge of two sets of parents and their extended families with her or his growing understanding of adoption.

Contact with the agency is likely to continue throughout the process. The need to feel free of agency "control" can become an issue.

Interventions

Much of the work with those involved in open adoption is likely to be ongoing, because of their commitment to a continuing relationship (contact, pictures, and letters). This ongoing relationship will involve special attention to record keeping, so that all agreements are clearly understood.

Early in the process, the adoption worker will need to clarify the issue of whose interests are to be represented. There is clearly a need for separate staff to be advocates for each party at some stage in the process. The child's own individual needs may need to be separately represented at a later stage.

Sessions with the extended families of birth parents and adoptive parents may be needed in order to assist them in understanding the meaning of open adoption, the responsibilities involved, roles and relationships, and future difficulties.

The adoption worker needs to have mediation skills in order to assist in conflict resolution and negotiation.

Birth parents who chose open adoption must not feel that their process of mourning the loss of their child will necessarily be more easily accomplished; in fact, it will require the same careful therapeutic attention as in a "closed adoption" (see chapter 4).

A life story book is useful for the adoptee, in which pictures and letters are stored to assist in the integration of significant people in his or her life.

TRANSRACIAL ADOPTION

Transracial adoption is an expanding area of adoption activity (Silverman, 1980). For the most part, transracial adoption refers to the placement of children from minority racial and ethnic backgrounds with Caucasian families. It also refers to the adoption of children of different nationalities from third world countries within Caucasian families.

The term "transracial adoption" is an all-encompassing designation. It refers to the situation in which white, usually middle class families adopt children of a different race (black or biracial). It also refers to the adoption of Asian children and children from other countries, who are sometimes identified as having been adopted "transculturally" or by means of "intercountry" adoption. Thus, intercountry adoption also involves the crossing of racial lines.

In-country transracial adoption has taken place for many years, while intercountry adoption has grown in popularity only over the last fifteen to twenty years.

Most of the intercountry adoptions involve children from countries such as Korea, Hong Kong, Latin and Central America, Sri Lanka, India and Vietnam. Some of these children are of mixed background and are called Eurasians. Only a small percentage of the adoptions are infant adoptions, and many of these children have been abandoned in early childhood. Sibling groups, older children, and those with some physical impairment are common. Many of the in-country children of minority group background have suffered some form of neglect and abuse.

Parents who adopt transracially are confronted with issues of race and culture not necessarily present in families with no racial diversity. Also, the children adopted transracially face identity issues substantially different from those facing in-racially adopted children. They are called upon to define their racial and ethnic identity and to integrate that self into Western culture. At the same time, they must turn to a foreign culture as they seek to define themselves and satisfy their curiosity about their biological heritage. Thus, both parents and child face complex issues of racial and ethnic allegiance.

It is a popular misconception that transracial adoption does not present a substantial barrier to bonding between the child and the adoptive parents. Research (Baldwin, 1984) indicates that while genetic factors alone do not determine relationships among family members, the fact of racial difference within a family has a profound and lasting effect.

Because racial difference is so visible, families who adopt transracially cannot escape community reaction and comment, nor can they escape the fact that their adopted child is not genetically tied to them. Because interracial families challenge society's taboo against the intermingling of races, these families may be unprepared for the bigotry and cultural and institutional racism to which they are often subjected (Baldwin, 1984).

Since most adoptive parents have not directly experienced racial discrimination prior to adopting transracially, they are often unprepared for the negative attitudes of relatives, neighbors, and friends. Also, some adoptive parents discover that they have underestimated how difficult it is to parent a child whose identity is so different from their own. This adjustment can be especially difficult when their original motivation to adopt was based on deep religious or humanitarian convictions.

Parental attitudes have a profound influence on the development of racial awareness in the adoptee. Jones and Else (1974) concluded that minority children raised by Caucasian parents are capable of developing a positive sense of racial identity. They stress, however, that there are some important attitudes and values which, if held by the adoptive parents, will make a substantial difference. These are:

1. a willingness to stand behind the adoptee in face of racism and racially-motivated attacks;
2. an awareness of their own racist attitudes and willingness to change them;
3. a sensitivity to racial and cultural differences;
4. a commitment to a way of life which allows their adopted children to be socialized into a minority culture.

Ladner (1977) emphasizes that, to be effective parents, Caucasian parents who adopt Black children must completely alter their values.

Some parents who adopt transracially assume, all too naively, that their love for their adopted child will be sufficient. However, with experience, they discover that their major parenting task consists of instilling in their adopted child a strong sense of racial and personal identity, without which the child will be overwhelmed as he or she grows up. Parental support for this socialization process is essential to the adoptee's self esteem and sense of social acceptance in the community.

A study of Asian adopted teenagers (Kim, 1977) reported that, while generally well adjusted , they showed signs of special vulnerability due to their dislike of their Asian features. Ironically, the adoptive parents in this study reported that they were unaware of the color or race of their children. This lack of awareness and failure to acknowledge real identity issues is cited as the reason these children feel they are more at risk. Kim believes that adoptive parents of Asian adopted children must resist "americanizing" their adopted children due to the fact that, more than anything else, they need a positive and strong sense of themselves as Asians. He notes that Asian adoptees who apparently lack interest in their cultural background may well be responding to mixed messages from their adoptive parents regarding the value of Asian culture.

Some families who adopt transracially place considerable emphasis on the importance of the foreign culture of the adoptee's motherland. This can be a helpful emphasis. However, it is also important for families to realize that, for example, it may be more helpful for their adopted son or daughter to have intimate contact with other Asian-Americans right at home, as they seek to understand where they fit into American society.

Case Example

The story of Siu Wai Anderson (Baldwin, 1984), a young Chinese American woman adopted transracially, illustrates the importance of this process.

In order to reclaim a part of her Asian identity, Sue Anderson changed her name as a young woman in 1978 to Sui Wai Anderson. Adopted at the age of two by an American family, she grew up with no contact with her Chinese mother. Sui Wai is the name her birth mother gave her as a baby and she now cherishes it. Sui Wai wrote a song to explain why she changed her name:

> Well, I've learned to like my face but I need to change my name
> To reflect the story hidden in my eyes
> You know I'll always keep the name of my family
> But now I see the dawn in the Asian skies (Baldwin, 1984, p. 1).

As Baldwin explains:

> "Sui Wai Anderson's name now communicates to others her sense of dual identity as an Asian and as an American. However, she did not always feel comfortable as the only Asian child growing up in a white family. Her song eloquently illustrates the dilemmas experienced by Asian children who have been adopted transracially. Her statement that she has "learned to like her face," indicates that there was a time when she did not appreciate the Asian features which singled her out as the object of teasing and racial taunts. In addition, the pictures in the family photo album were constant reminders to her of the fact that she was adopted, that she did not belong to the family in the same way as her Caucasian American siblings did.
> Whereas Sui Wai had felt isolated as the only Asian child in a white family, as a young adult she experienced the feeling of not belonging to the Chinese-American community because she was not familiar with Chinese cultural traditions or language. Her Asian features identified her as a member of the community, but her experience classified her as part of the white majority culture. Her heritage as an Asian person had little significance for her until she was ready to reclaim her identity as a Chinese-American.
> At the age of twenty she began to establish some connections to the local Asian community. She lived in Chinatown in San Franciso for several years, where she learned to speak Cantonese. Moreover she gained some insight into the lives of other Chinese-American people, a different experience from her white middle class upbringing. Thus she began the process of reconciliation between the psycho-social self she had developed in her white American home, and the physical self she had inherited from her Chinese ancestors.
> ... (Sui Wai) felt she could not move forward until she had put down some roots

in the "rich Asian earth" of her Chinese heritage. As she indicates in her song:
You've got to know where you're from to know
Where you want to go and I think I'll be going home
One of these days.
When Sui Wai speaks of "going home;" she does not mean it in the literal sense of going back to Hong Kong where she was born (at least not for now) but the phrase does express her desire to complete the missing portion of her life story ... Sui Wai's adoption story does not include the first two years of her life.
... the resolution of identity she has achieved in her early twenties may dissolve in the face of a future crises. Adoption issues in particular seem to resurface at critical moments of passage from one life stage to the next ...
Sui Wai's story is representative of an Asian adopted person's perspective on transracial Asian adoption ... namely, the struggles to define racial and ethnic identity, to integrate the experiences of the Asian self and the American self, to explore personal roots in Asian culture; and, for some, to extend that exploration to include a search for their Asian birth parents (Baldwin, 1984 pp. 1/5).

Clinical Issues

Families that adopt transracially are making a decision which truly has life long implications. It is a decision that will effect not only their family unit but also generations to come.

Parents who adopt transracially will be subject to both criticism and support. Their motives will be challenged by both close friends and the outside community.

Their adopted children's understanding of their racial identity will consist of a developmental process. For example, while Asian adoptees are not particularly interested in their ethnic background during the early years, this changes dramatically as they become young adults. As young adults they want to know about their Asian roots and begin to see themselves as "Asian-Americans" (Baldwin, 1984). As noted earlier, families who adopt transracially may believe that intensive exposure to cultural activities which focus on the native land (such as visits to galleries and attendance at "Korea day" activities) are sufficient. The evidence indicates that intimate contact with other Asian-Americans or other Black-Americans is also very helpful to identify formation.

Children adopted transracially find security initially in the acceptance they receive from their families, without an emphasis on how dissimilar they are from other family members (Baldwin, 1984). As they enter school, leave the home and begin to face racial discrimination they often need support from their parents in learning how to protect themselves.

Because the birth parents are in a distant land, it is sometimes assumed that the family is essentially helpless in seeking contact with or without information about them. While this may be true in some cases, it is often possible to secure more information and even hold out the hope of contact. This may require a determined effort by the family.

Some families can be prone to minimize the importance of the birth parents in their child's life. This tendency may be based, in part, on the family's uncertainty about how to handle information they regard as potentially negative. Although many transracially adopted children are still considered to have been "abandoned" (babies left anonymously at an orphanage or with the police), this does not necessarily preclude a successful search leading to contact.

Intervention

Most of the interventions described earlier in this chapter as appropriate for special needs adoption are relevant to the transracial adoption area. Those more specifically relevant to transracial adoption are:

1. Assisting the family as they face issues of race and racism which, in many instances, are unexpected and for which they may be unprepared.
2. Responding to the family's needs as they cope with the child's early adjustment, especially if the child is older (problems such as language and food differences).
3. Helping the family to cope with their child's anger and frustration over having been separated from his family of origin and his culture.
4. Educating the family about how to approach the agency or international organization for more information about both the circumstances of their child's birth and the possible whereabouts of the birth parents.
5. Family sessions may be helpful as the family seeks to build upon and consolidate their identity as a family. This may be facilitated by incorporating new rituals and traditions into the pattern of family life.
6. Encouraging the family to join self-help groups where they are able to gain further insight and support.
7. Participating in special workshops such as "Understanding Transracial Adoption" (first presented by the Post Adoption Center for Education and Research and Holt International Children's Services, 1983) can be especially useful, both to families considering transracial adoption and those who have already adopted. Such workshops present a holistic view of the adoption experience and provide insights otherwise not easily obtained. (A report on the workshop, including summaries of presentations by adoptive parents, birth parents, and adoptees who have experienced transracial adoption, is contained in Baldwin (1984), *An exploration of the needs and concerns of Caucasian families who have*

adopted Asian children. [Unpublished Master's Thesis, San Francisco Theological Seminary, San Anselmo, CA 94960]. This report can be obtained by writing Margaret Baldwin, 1192 West San Jose, Fresno, CA 93711.)

ARTIFICIAL INSEMINATION BY DONOR (AID) AND SURROGATE MOTHERHOOD

Among the growing number of alternative methods of reproduction, we will consider only two of the most prominent: artificial insemination by donor (AID) and surrogacy, more commonly referred to as "surrogate motherhood."

AID has been practiced for many years whereas surrogacy is a relatively new procedure. While there are perhaps only 1,000 surrogate births to date in the United States, it is estimated that 250,000 (Annas, 1980) children are conceived by means of AID each year in the U.S..

How does AID work? AID is most often employed by an infertile couple in which the husband is infertile. The female partner is inseminated with the sperm of an anonymous donor. The female partner conceives and gives birth to the child, and the child is then assumed to be the couple's child. The sperm donor (actually he is a "sperm vendor," for he is most often paid for his services) is guaranteed complete anonymity by the infertility clinic or sperm bank (Annas, 1980). Professional donors are often used for multiple inseminations; the husband's and the donor's semen are sometimes mixed at the time of insemination. Single women are increasingly turning to AID; many are inseminating themselves at home with sperm donated by a friend.

We need to state our concerns regarding both AID and surrogacy from the outset. Although we do not include a review of the moral, ethical, and legal issues which are being raised with respect to surrogacy and AID (Annas, 1987; Davis & Brown, 1987; Gould, 1987), we do present a discussion of the critical clinical issues facing all the parties involved.

One of the most significant issues in the practice of AID is that the identity of the sperm donor is forever sealed. No matter how serious a concern might develop with respect to the AID child's emotional or physical health, the child and his or her family are unable to gain access to information about health problems which may have emerged in the life of the sperm donor and are, therefore, relevant to the well-being of the AID produced child.

Another issue is the fact that the AID family must cope with the fact that their child is a product of someone else's sperm — a fact that is most often kept secret by AID families. Living with a secret of such significance for the family places a special burden on the entire family system. Unlike the adopted child, the AID family is forever denied personal contact with and access to vital information about the sperm donor to whom the AID child is genetically tied (Davis & Brown, 1984).

Surrogacy presents an even more complex set of problems. Surrogacy is a process whereby a woman (referred to as the "surrogate mother") signs a contract to conceive, give birth to, and relinquish her child to an infertile couple, usually for the sum of $10,000 or more. The surrogate mother is then inseminated with the sperm of the husband of the infertile couple. The contract specifies that the surrogate mother must relinquish the child for adoption by the contracting couple immediately upon delivery.

The woman who signs a contract to become a surrogate mother is often compared with the birth mother who relinquishes her child for adoption. However, there is a significant difference: in surrogacy the pregnancy is intentional; in adoption, the pregnancy is usually unintended. Surrogacy presents the "surrogate birth mother" with an even more problematic set of life course issues (guilt, shame, grief) than those facing relinquishing mothers through adoption. Unlike the relinquishing mother in adoption, the surrogate mother must live with the fact that she was paid to bear her child. Some segments of the community regard this as baby selling.

We believe it is impossible for the surrogate mother to anticipate all the feelings that will arise during her pregnancy, the birth, and the relinquishment process. Therefore, the notion of signing a contract binding her to this commitment is inviting substantial difficulty and long term dysfunction for all concerned.

As we noted in chapter 1, adoption practice has shifted from a focus on meeting the needs of infertile couples to meeting the needs of the child. AID and surrogacy both represent a return to that outmoded emphasis, because they are concerned with satisfying the unmet needs of the individuals rather than the child so produced.

The potential for family dysfunction and impaired adjustment of all those involved in AID and surrogacy (Snowden & Mitchell, 1981; Davis & Brown, 1984) has been the subject of extended study and commentary.

Our primary concern throughout this book is the long term effects of these practices on all the parties involved: the surrogate mother, the family of the surrogate mother (her husband, other children, her parents), the couple who contracts for her services, and, most important, the child her- or himself. From our clinical experience in the field of adoption, we are able to predict that there will be social and emotional problems facing the AID and surrogacy-produced child.

Although many of the clinical issues discussed in chapter 3 are relevant here, the following clinical issues deserve special attention as they relate to AID and surrogacy.

ARTIFICIAL INSEMINATION BY DONOR

Clinical Issues

Secrecy

AID families must engage in continuing and covert subterfuge (Snowden & Mitchell, 1981) as they conceal the true nature of their child's origins and genetic birthright. The negative effects of a family secret of this magnitude are well documented (Snowden & Mitchell, 1981). Keeping such a secret, all the time fearing disclosure, invites family stress, anxiety, and dysfunction.

Betrayal and Lack of Trust

Although most AID children are raised with no knowledge of their full genetic heritage, it is not uncommon for the AID child to sense that something is being withheld — that something is different about his or her family and relationship to it. When discovering the truth sometime later in life, AID children report (Davis & Brown, 1984) a profound sense of having been betrayed and great difficulty in ever trusting their parents.

Davis and Brown (1984) report two cases:

> Case 1. The woman was 31 years old when she found that she was an AID child. Learning at 31 that her father was a sperm donor she felt resentment against her parents and blamed an unhappy childhood on their inability to cope with the AID. "Living the big lie warped and poisoned the relationship beyond repair." After her mother died, the woman's father finally told her she was an AID child. "You have to understand that to my father the fact that my mother was impregnated by another man was an ugly secret. His infertility was an ugly secret. It was something to be ashamed of." Her feelings about her discovery are portrayed in her comments about the sperm donor:
> "I wanted to know how he could have sold what was the essence of my life for $25 to a total stranger, then walk away without a second thought. I wanted to know why he didn't have the maturity to think about me ... why couldn't he connect the semen to the human being it would create?"
> Case 2. This woman was 33 years old in 1981 when she wrote the following:
> "I have been denied knowledge of my birth father because of artificial insemination in 1948. My parents divorced shortly afterward and I grew up basically without a father. I wonder how many (hundreds?) of brothers and sisters I have? I wonder if my children will ever run into their aunts and uncles and cousins unbeknownst to me? I have so many unmet questions and needs. I wish there could be some publicity about this and encourage donors to come forward and register — if their children wish to know of their heredity" (p. 128).

Genetic Ties and Family Imbalance

The fact that the AID child is genetically tied to the woman but not to the man is a basis for marital tension and dysfunction. This imbalance in the relationship can be further complicated if the couple has not resolved their infertility issues.

Intervention

The initial goal of therapy with prospective AID parents is to attend to their immediate needs. These may consist of unfinished grief work over their infertility, and options other than AID can be explored. However, if they decide to proceed with AID, the short and long term implications need to be explored — the effects on the child, their ability to handle the secrecy, and the need to cope with the fact that they will never be able to provide their child with information about his genetic heritage. They will need to consider how they will respond should their child suspect that he or she is not genetically related to his or her father. The prospective AID couple must also face the fact that they will not be able to know with certainty what inherited diseases may emerge in their child's life, such as cancer, heart disease, and alcohol and drug dependency (Goodwin, 1985; Cadoret, O'Gorman, Troughton & Heywood, 1985).

AID children who seek therapy as adults and who suspect something has been withheld by their family, will need help in dealing with their rage over having been misled and their sense of subsequent alienation from their parents. They will also need help in coping with their rage toward their sperm-donating father and their feelings of abandonment. The therapeutic task will be one of integrating into their lives the reality of these discoveries about their identity. Issues of identity, trust, and potential vulnerability to disease and other genetic characteristics will be of primary concern.

SURROGACY

Clinical issues

The clinical issues for the surrogate mother are both short and long term. In the short term, she must attempt to come to terms with what it means for her and her family to agree to sign a contract to relinquish without knowing how she will feel during her pregnancy. She must also evaluate, for herself and her family, the long-term implications of the fact that her contact with the child will be limited once the child is placed in the home of the contracting couple. She will need to consider the impact of the separation she and every birth parent experiences, but with the added complications in this case of having accepted money as a part of the contract. The surrogate mother and her family are in the difficult position of needing to weigh the emotional risks of signing a contract when they really cannot know for certain

Special Issues in Adoption

in advance how this decision will effect their family down through the years. She will need to consider the effect of her decision on others in her family, especially if there are existing children who may be concerned that they, too, might be abandoned.

Looking even further ahead, the surrogate mother will need to prepare for the time when (perhaps 15 years or more after she relinquishes the child) she may be reunited with her surrogate child (now an adult).

The primary clinical issues facing the surrogate child will be the burden of living with the "story" of his or her conception and birth (e.g., that he was paid for by his father and sold by his mother, that his biological father and mother are in two separate families, and that he is separated from his half brothers and sisters because of the surrogacy arrangement.)

From a life course perspective, all of those involved (the surrogate mother, her husband, their children; the couple who pay for the child) will potentially live with issues of uncertainty about the wisdom of their decision, unexpected feelings of guilt, shame, and loss, and potential confusion about roles and relationships during the years ahead.

Surrogacy places all those involved in a position of social and emotional risk and vulnerability.

Intervention

The focus of therapy with families considering surrogacy will depend upon the particular stage of decision making. Interventions in working with the infertile couple may include:

1. An assessment of their readiness to enter into a contract which may not be fulfilled (Davis & Brown, 1987; Gould, 1987; Annas, 1987) due to a change of heart on the part of the surrogate mother.
2. An exploration of how prepared they feel they will be in helping their child live with the story of how he or she was produced.
3. Exploring with the couple the full and continuing impact on their relationship of the fact that their child is genetically only "half theirs."
4. Helping the couple anticipate, and assess their readiness to withstand, the public criticism they may well encounter as participants in such a controversial practice.

The focus of therapy with the surrogate mother and her family will also depend on the stage they are in with respect to the decision making process. Potential interventions will consist of:

1. Assisting the surrogate mother in the process of making such a decision for herself and her entire family.

2. Encouraging the surrogate mother, her husband and children to explore all the issues together in family therapy.

Chapter 8
The Future

We are optimistic about the future. Post-adoption services are expanding and in some areas flourishing. It was only a few years ago that the need for post-adoption services began to be recognized. Much of the impetus has come from the widespread growth of triad search and support groups, and recognition that adoption is a life course reality for hundreds of thousands of persons and their extended families.

The earlier hostility between groups advocating "open records" and the "adoption establishment" has tended to moderate. Today there is much more communication and collaboration between self-help and professional groups. We see this trend continuing.

The growth of self help and advocacy groups has enabled scores of triad members to know each other. As search and reunion activity continues to become even more widespread, the sense of isolation and alienation among and between members of the adoption triad has diminished considerably.

Deeply imbedded stereotypes about adoption are beginning to fall by the wayside. More and more lay persons and professionals are developing an awareness and understanding of the adoption experience. They are recognizing one simple truth about adoption: it is different. Not "good different" or "bad different", just different.

There is an encouraging trend today toward preventive services. This is reflected in a recognition of the importance of pre-adoptive counseling and education for adoptive parents and pre-relinquishment counseling for birth parents. Ongoing support for birth parents during the post-relinquishment period is another significant development. Agencies are now more ready to maintain contact with their adoptive families after finalization. We believe it will become even more important in the future.

Openness in adoption will continue to be a subject of widespread interest — open records, open adoption, and other forms of openness among members of the adoption triad. The adoption reform movement will continue to pursue its quest for open records. Open adoption, as practiced by private or independent (non-agency— adoption practitioners in the U.S.), will continue to flourish as the most popular method of adoption in states which legally permit it. What we do not know is what the long term effects of open adoption will be on the child. Longitudinal research on the outcome of open adoption practice is needed.

In the area of independent and private adoption, there is a continuing need for better integration of the clinical and legal aspects of the process, with attorneys and clinicians achieving more effective means of collaboration in the interest of their clients.

There continues to be an unmet need for the rigorous assessment of various adoption practices. Some of the important research topics requiring exploration are the long term outcomes of search and post-reunion adjustment; the outcome of access legislation and its use in the design of improved placement practices; and the evaluation of various types of care arrangements in the area of special needs adoption. Finally, there is a need for the development and evaluation of various therapeutic modes, relevant to children with attachment difficulties.

We are concerned for parents whose parental rights have been (or will be) terminated; few appear to be receiving therapeutic services and support. They will go on to have other children whose siblings are in permanent care.

The long-term outcomes of the new birth technologies (in particular, AID and surrogacy) need to be clearly established, and appropriate services need to be developed for those affected.

Adoption practices and the needs of those involved will continue to change; post adoption services must be able to respond to the changing face of adoption.

References

Andrews, G., Tennant, C., Hewson, D. M., & Vaillant, G. E. (1978). Life events stress, social support, coping style, and risk of psychological impairment. *The Journal of Nervous and Mental Disease, 166,* 307-316.

Annas, G. J. (1987). Baby M: babies and justice for sale. *Hastings Center Report,* June 1987, 13-15.

Annas, G. J. (1980). Fathers anonymous: beyond the best interests of the sperm donor. *Family Law Quarterly, 14,* 1-13.

Backhaus, K. (1984). Life books: Tool for working with children in placement. *Social Work, 29*(6), 551-554.

Baldwin, M. L. (1984). *An exploration of the needs of caucasian families who have adopted Asian children: A workshop model.* Unpublished master's thesis, San Francisco Theological Seminary, San Anselmo, CA.

Benet, M. K. (1970). *The politics of adoption.* New York: Free Press.

Blum, L. (1976). When adoptive families ask for help. *Primary Care, 3* 242-249.

Bourguignon, J. P., & Watson, K. (1987a). *After adoption: a manual for professionals working with adoptive families.* Chicago: Illinois Department of Children and Family Services.

Bourguignon, J. P., & Watson, K. (1987b). *After adoption: a training guide.* Chicago: Illinois Department of Children and Family Services.

Brodzinsky, D. M. (1984). New perspectives on adoption revelation. *Early Child Development & Care, 18*(1-2) 105-118.

Brodzinsky, D. M. (1986). Adjustment to adoption: a psychosocial perspective. *Clinical Psychology Review, 7,* 25-47.

Brodzinsky, D. M. (1987). Adjustment to adoption: A psychosocial perspective. *Clinical Psychology Review. 7* 25 47.

Brodzinsky, D. M., Pappas, C., Singer, L. M., & Braff, A. M. (1981). Children's conception of adoption: A preliminary investigation. *Journal of Pediatric Psychology. 6*(2), 177-189.

Brodzinsky, D. M., Schechter, D. E., Baff, A. M., & Singer, L. M. (1984). Psychological and academic adjustment in adopted child. *Journal of Consulting and Clinical Psychology, 52,* 582-590.

Brodzinsky, D. M., Singer, L. M., & Braff, A. M. (1984). Children's understanding of adoption. *Child Development, 55*(3) 869-78.

Brown, D. W. (Ed.) (1981). *Dialogue for understanding: a handbook for adoptive and pre-adoptive parents.* Palo Alto, CA: Post Adoption Center for Education and Research.

Brown, D. W. (1983). *Handbook of the post adoption center for education and research: A guide to the programs, services, and structure of a community-based organization known as PACER*. Orient, NY: Author.
Brown, G. W., & Harris, T. (1978). *The social origins of depression*. London: Tavistock.
Cadoret, R. J., O'Gorman, T. W., Troughton, E., & Heywood, E. (1985). Alcoholism and antisocial personality. *Archives of General Psychiatry, 42*, 161-167.
Children's Home Society of Minnesota, 1984. *Model Statement on Post-Legal Adoption Services*, St. Paul, MN: Author.
Condon, J. (1986). Psychological disability in women who relinquish a baby for adoption. *Medical Journal of Australia, 177*, 117-119.
Connor, T., Sclare, I., Dunbar, D., Elliffe, J. (1985). Making a life story book. *Adoption and Fostering, 9*(2), 32-35, 46.
Davis, J. H. (1979). The pediatric role in adoption. *Clinical Pediatrics, 18* (7), 439-443.
Davis, J. H., & Brown, D. W. (1981). Adoption: pediatric, legislative, and social issues (issues in medicine). *Western Journal of Medicine, 135*(1), 72-77.
Davis, J. H., & Brown, D. W. (1984). Artificial insemination by donor (AID) and the use of surrogate mothers: social and psychological impact. *Western Journal of Medicine, 141*(1), 127-130.
Davis, J. H., Brown, D. W. (1987). Surrogacy is a mistake. *Sonoma County Physician*, 38(10) 7-8.
Derdeyn, A. P. (1979). Adoption and the ownership of children. *Child Psychiatry and Human Development, 9* 119-136.
Derdeyn, A. P. (1980). Adoption. In Schetky, D. H. & Benedek, E. P. (Eds.), *Child psychiatry and the law*. New York: Brunner/Mazel.
Deutsch, C. K., Swanson, J. M., Bruell, J. H., Cantwell, D. P., Weinberg, F., & Baren, M. (1982). Overrepresentation of adoptees in children with the attention deficit disorder. *Behavioral Genetics, 12*(2), 231-238.
Deykin, E. Y., Campbell, L., & Path, P. (1984). The post-adoption experience of surrendering parents. *American Journal of Orthopsychiatry, 54*(2), 271-280.
Erikson, E. (1963). *Childhood and society* (2nd ed.). New York: W. W. Norton.
Erikson, E. (1968). *Identity: youth and crisis*. New York: W. W. Norton.
Fisher, F. (1973). *The search for Anna Fisher*. New York: Arthur Fields.
Floud, C. (1982). The adoption triangle. *Adoption & Fostering, 6*(4), 50-52.
Fonda, A. (1984). *Birth mothers who search: an exploratory study*. Unpublished doctoral dissertation, California School of Professional Psychology, Berkeley, CA.
Goodwin, D. W., (1985). Alcoholism and genetics. *Archives of General Psychiatry, 42*, 171-174.
Gould, R. E., 1987. And what about Baby M's ruined life? *The New York Times*, op-ed page, Section 1, p. 27.
Grabe, P. (Ed). (1986). *Adoption resources for mental health professionals*. Mercer, PA: Children's Aid Society.
Hartman, A. (1979). *Finding families: an ecological approach to family assessment in adoption*. Beverly Hills, CA: Sage Publications.
Hartman, A. (1984). *Working with adoptive families beyond placement*. New York: Child Welfare League of America.
Inglis, K. D. (1984). *Living mistakes: mothers who consented to adoption*. Sydney: George Allen and Unwin.
Jewett, C. L. (1982). *Helping children cope with separation and loss*. Harvard, MA: Harvard Commons Press.
Jones, C. E., & Else, J. F. (1974). Racial and cultural issues in adoption. *Child Welfare, 58*, 373-382.

References

Kent, K.G., & Richie, J. L. (1976). Adoption as an issue in casework with adoptive parents. *Journal of the American Academy of Child psychiatry, 133*(10), 1134-1136.

Kim, D. S. (1979). How they fared in American homes: A follow-up study of adopted Korean children. *Children Today,* 6(2), 2-6.

Kirk, H. D. (1984). *Shared fate: A theory and method of adoptive relationships* (Rev. Ed.). Brentwood Bay, Canada: Ben-Simon Publications.

Kirk, H. D. (1985) (Rev. Ed.). *Adoptive kinship — a modern institution in need of reform.* Brentwood Bay, Canada: Ben-Simon Publications.

Knight, R. P. (1941). Some problems involved in selecting and rearing an adopted child. *Child Adoption,* 62(4), 27-35.

Kraft, A. D., Palombo, J., Mitchell, D., Dean, C., Meyers, S., & Wright, A. W. (1980). The psychological dimensions of infertility. *American Journal of Orthopsychiatry, 50,* 618-628.

Ladner, J. (1977). *Mixed families.* New York: Anchor Press.

Lawton, J. J., & Goss, S. Z. (1964). Review of psychiatric literature on adopted children. *Archives of General Psychiatry, 11,* 635-644.

Lifton, B. J. (1975). *Twice born: Memoirs of an adopted daughter.* New York: Dial Press.

Lifton, B. J. (1979). *Lost and found: the adoption experience.* New York: Dial Press.

McHutchison, J. (1986). *Relinquishing a child: the circumstances and effect of loss.* Unpublished Bachelor of Social Science thesis, University of New South Wales, Australia.

McWinnie, A. (1967). *Adopted children and how they grow up.* London: Routledge and Kegan Paul.

Melina, L. R. (1986). *Raising adopted children: a manual for adoptive parents.* New York: Harper and Row.

Menning, B. E. (1977). *Infertility: a guide for the childless couple.* Englewood Cliffs, NJ: Prentice-Hall.

Midford, S. (1986). *The development of a model and measure of adoptee identity.* Unpublished master's dissertation, University of Tasmania, Australia.

Midford, S. (1987). A measure of adoptee identity. *Uniview* 6(1), 8-9.

Post Adoption Center for Education and Research. (PACER). Workshop for birthparents: "Healing Ourselves." Walnut Creek, CA: Author.

Pannor, R., & Nerlove, E. A. (1977). Fostering understanding between adolescents and adoptive parents through group experiences. *Child Welfare, 56,* 537-545.

Paton, J. M. (1954). *Adoptees break silence.* Action, CA: Life History Study Center.

Renne, D. (1977). "There's always adoption": The infertility problem. *Child Welfare,* 56(7) 465-471.

Reynearson, E. (1982). Relinquishment and its maternal complications: a preliminary study. *American Journal of Psychiatry, 139* (3), 338-340.

Rillera, M. J. (1981). *The adoption searchbook: techniques for tracing people.* Huntington Beach, CA: Triadoption Publications.

Schechter, M. D. (1960). Observations on adopted children. *Archives of General Psychiatry,* 3, 21-22.

Silverman, A. R. (1980). *Transracial adoption in the United States: A study of assimilation and adjustment.* Unpublished doctoral dissertation, University of Wisconsin, Madison.

Small, J. W. (1987). Working with adoptive families. *Public Welfare,* Summer 1987, 41-48.

Snowden, R., & Mitchell, G. D. (1981). *The artificial family: A consideration of artificial insemination by donor.* London: George Allen and Unwin.

Sorosky, A. D., Baran, A., & Pannor, R. (1978). *The adoption triangle.* New York: Anchor.

Triseliotis, J. (1973). *In search of origins: The experience of adopted people.* Boston: Beacon Press.

Winkler, R., and van Keppel, M. (1984). *Relinquishing mothers in adoption: their long-term adjustment.* Melbourne, Australia: Institute of Family Studies.

Suggested Readings

Ahmed, S., Cheetham, J., & Small, J. (eds.) (1986). *Working with black children and their families.* London: British Agencies for Adoption and Fostering.
Adoption Legislation Review Committee, *Report of the Adoption Legislation Review Committee.* Melbourne: Victorian Government Printing Office.
Begley, O., Murr, A., Springen, K., Gordon, J. & Harrison, J. (November 23, 1987) All about twins. *Newsweek.* pp. 58-69.
Benet, H. K. (1976). *The Politics of adoption.* New York: The Free Press.
Bouchard, T. J., Jr. (1984). Twins reared apart and together: What they tell us about human diversity. In S. W. Fox (ed.), *Individuality and determinism.* New York: Plenum.
Brown, C. (1984). *Healing ourselves: a workshop for birthparents, by birthmothers.* Walnut Creek, CA: Post Adoption Center for Education and Research (PACER).
Condon, J. (1986). Psychological disability in women who relinquish a baby for adoption. *Medical Journal of Australia, 177,* 117-119.
Corea, G. (1985). *The mother machine.* New York: Harper & Row.
Dusky, L. (1979). *Birthmark.* New York: Mark Evans and Co.
Feigelman, W., & Silverman, A. S. (1983). *Chosen children: new patterns of adoptive relationships.* New York: Praeger.
Gill, O., & Jackson, B. (1983). *Adoption and race: black, Asian, and mixed race children in white families.* New York: St. Martin's Press.
Harper, J. (1986). An individual at risk? The adopted adolescent and family. *Australian Social Work, 39* (i), 9-13.
Hoksbergen, R. A. C. (1986). *Adoption in worldwide perspective: A review of programs, policies and legislation in 14 countries.* Berwyn, PA: Swets North American Inc.
Karpel, M. A. (1980). Family secrets: I. Conceptual and ethical issues in the relational context; II. Ethical and practical considerations in therapeutic

management. Family Process, 19, 295–306.

Kline, N. J. (1984). *A study of adult adoptees: self concepts and attitudes toward adoptive mothers with emphasis on the effects of reunion with birthparent(s).* Unpublished dissertation, California School of Marital and Family Therapy, Hayward, CA.

Krementz, J. (1982). *How it feels to be adopted.* New York: Alfred A. Knopf.

Livingston, C. (1978). *Why was I adopted?* Sydney: Angus and Robertson.

May, E. (1986). *Tell me my story: a book for adopted children, their parents and friends.* Blackburn: Dove Communications.

McRoy, R. G., & Zurcher, L. A., Jr. (1983). *Transracial and inracial adoptees: the adolescent years.* Springfield Il: Charles C. Thomas.

Melina, L. (1986). *Raising adopted children: a manual for adoptive parents.* New York: Harper & Row.

Melina, L. (ed.) *Adopted child newsletter,* P.O. Box 9362, Moscow, Idaho 83843.

Nerlove, E. (1985). *Who is David? The story of an adopted adolescent and his friends.* New York: Child Welfare League of America.

Paton, J. M. (1968). *Orphan Voyage.* New York: Vantage.

Rillera, M. J. (1987). *Adoption encounter: hurt, transition, healing.* Westminster, CA: Triadoption Publications.

Shawyer, J. (1979). *Death by adoption.* Auckland: Cicada Press.

Silbert, K., and Speedlin, P. (1983). *Dear birthmother.* San Antonio TX: Corona Publishing Co.

Silverman, P. (1981). *Helping women cope with grief.* Beverly Hills, CA: Sage Publications.

Slaytor, P. (1986). Reunion and resolution: the adoption triangle. *Australian Social Work, 39*(2), 15–20.

Snow, R. (Ed.) (1983). *Understanding adoption: a practical guide.* Sydney: Fontana Books.

Spencer, M. (1979) The terminology of adoption. *Child Welfare,* 451–459.

van Keppel, M. (1986). How dare they? The experiences of women who have relinquished children for adoption and the tasks of intervention. In, *Proceedings of the Fourth National Women and Therapy Conference,* Perth, Australia.

Winkler, R., and Midford, S. (1986). Biological identity in adoption, artificial insemination by donor (A.I.D.) and the new birth technologies. *Australian Journal of Early Childhood, 11* (4).

Glossary of Terms and Phrases

The following terms and phrases, most of which are peculiar to the adoption arena, are defined below to assist the reader:

Adoptee — the person who is relinquished by the birth parents and placed into the adoptive home, becoming the parenting responsibility of the adoptive parents.

Adoptive parents — the individuals (usually, but not always, a couple) who legally adopt the child and raise the child in the context of their family.

Adoption triad — refers to all three parties to an adoption: the two birth parents, the two adoptive parents, and the adoptee (single parent adoptions are included).

Birth parents — the mother and father responsible for the conception, birth, and placement of the adopted child.

Extended adoption family — includes those primarily involved (e.g., the adoption triad) and all of the people related to members of the triad, such as children, siblings, aunts, uncles, grandparents, cousins, and others.

Infertile couple — the couple that is unable to conceive and give birth to a child because of physical and/or emotional impairment.

Non-identifying information — the information collected and recorded about the adoptee during the process of adoption which is later made available to the parties involved should they request it. It is "non-identifying" in that all references to actual names and places, are withheld to insure the anonymity of those involved.

Open adoption — defines the pre- and post-placement process, whereby the birth parents and adoptive parents have personal contact with each other. In many cases the birth parents actually select the adoptive parents with whom their child will be placed, and open adoption usually denotes continuing post-placement contact between birth parents, and adoptive parents and the adoptee. (There are degress of "openness," ranging from limited contact to an on-going relationship including the exchange of letters, pictures, and so forth.

Relinquishment — the last step in the decision-making process of the birth parents which results in the placement of the child with the adoptive family.

Search — the process wherein the adoptee seeks information about and contact with his or her birth parents. The same term is used when birth parents seek contact with the child they relinquished.

Reunion — the end point of the search process when the searching person locates and has personal contact with (sometimes it is over the telephone) the person(s) for whom he/she has been searching.

Sealed adoption records — When the adopted child is placed with the adoptive parents, the original birth certificate is sealed by the courts and a new birth certificate is issued. Access to the sealed record is possible only under court order in most U. S. states.

Special needs adoption — refers to the adoption of children who have experienced some trauma (abuse, neglect), multiple placements, developmental disabilities, or intellectual or physical impairment.

Traditional adoption — the process whereby the adopted child is placed in the adoptive home without prior contact between the birth parents and adoptive parents and with none of the parties having access to identifying information about each other.

The adoption movement — the organized effort by adoptees and birth parents, with the participation of some adoptive parents, adoption professionals, and others to support each other locally and unite nationally for legislative reform (from sealed to open records), education, program development, and mutual support.

Author Index

Andrews, G., 54
Annas, G., 113, 117

Backhaus, 89, 103, 183
Baldwin, M., 47, 108, 110, 111, 112–113
Baran, A., 18, 19, 45, 70
Baren, M., 38
Benet, M. K., 19
Blum, L., 70
Bourguignon, J. P., 27, 36, 37, 38, 103, 104, 105
Braff, A. M., 76
Brodzinsky, D., 20, 69, 73, 76, 78, 86, 87, 89
Brown, D. W., 28, 45, 47, 70, 113, 114, 115, 117
Brown, G. W., 54
Bruell, J. H., 38

Cadoret, R. J., 116
Campbell, L., 48
Cantwell, D. P., 38
Children's Home Society of Minnesota, 23
Condon, J., 48
Connor, T., 89, 103

Davis, J. H., 20, 47, 113, 114, 115, 117
Dean, C., 70
Derdeyn, A. P., 70
Deutsch, C. K., 38
Deykin, E. Y., 48
Dunbar, D., 103

Elliffe, J., 103
Else, J. F., 109
Erickson, E., 85, 89

Fisher, F., 19, 45–46
Floud, C., 26, 42
Fonda, A., 48

Gill, O., 46–47
Goodwin, D. W., 116
Gould, R. E., 113, 117
Grabe, P., 27, 37, 41, 104
Gross, S. Z., 75

Hartman, A., 37, 38
Hewson, D. M., 54
Heywood, E., 116
Hoksbergen, R. A. C., 93
Holt International Children's Services, 112

Inglis, K. D., 46, 48
International Soundex Reunion Registry, 93

Jackson, B., 46–47
Jewett, C. L., 46, 101, 103
Jones, C. E., 109

Kent, K. G., 70
Kim, D. S., 109

Kirk, H. D., 18, 19, 46, 69, 73, 80
Knight, R. P., 75
Kral, A. D., 70
Krementz, J., 46

Ladner, J., 109
Lawton, J. J., 75
Lifton, B. J., 19, 45, 46, 26, 75, 89, 94
Lifton, R. J., 20

McHutchinson, J., 48
McWinnine, A., 19
McRoy, R., 47
Melina, L. R., 46, 102, 103, 104
Meyers, S., 70
Midford, S., 20, 36, 89
Mitchell, D., 47, 114, 115

Nerlove, E. A., 80

O'Gorman, T. W., 116

Palombo, J., 70
Pannor, R., 18, 19, 45, 70, 80
Pappas, C., 76
Path, P., 48
Patti, P., 48
Paton, J. M., 19
Post Adoption Center for Education and Research (PACER), 41, 46, 66, 112

Renne, D., 70
Reynearson, E., 48
Richie, J. L., 70

Schechter, M. D., 75
Sclare, I., 103
Shawyer, 64
Silverman, A. R., 64, 107
Singer, L. M., 76
Small, J., 70, 82, 83, 85, 90, 92, 97
Sorosky, A. D., 18, 19, 45, 70
Snow, R., 45
Snowden, R., 47, 114, 115
Swanson, J. M., 38

Tennent, 54
Triseliotis, J., 18, 19
Troughton, E., 116

van Keppel, M., 20, 46, 48, 53
Vaillant, G. E., 54

Winkler, R., 20, 46, 48, 53
Watson, K., 27, 36, 37, 38, 103, 104, 105
Wright, A. W., 70

Zurcher, L. A., 47

Subject Index

Abandonment
  fear of, 87, 97
Adaptive grieving, 78, 88
Adoptee
  adolescence, 89
  adulthood, 90
  and denial, 90–92, 97
  and identity, 89–90
  case study, 87–89, 95–96
  decision to search, 91
  fantasies, 11
  goals of intervention, 98
  infancy, 85
  process of search, 93–94
  reunion, 94
  search and reunion, 91
  school age years, 86
  stages of development, 85–91
  stages of search, 94
  stages of letting go of denial, 90–91
  therapeutic considerations, 97
  toddlerhood and preschool period, 85
  value of self-help groups, 98
Adoptee Liberty Movement Association (ALMA), 6, 43
Adoptee's story
  elements of, 98
Adoption
  agencies, 2
  and alienation, 5
  and fear and hostility, 5
  and life course perspective, xv
  and loss, 31
  as a risk factor, xvi, 3
  and secrets, 5
  changing focus of, 1
  current scene, 20–21
  denial of difference, 9
  difficulties arising from, 2
  false premises, 5
  future of, 119
  incidence of, 3
  international scene, 17
  need for service, 21
  stereotypes in, 33
Adoption community
  common interests, 14
  defined, 6, 14
Adoption practice
  changes in, 9, 100–101
  current scene, 20
  integration of services, 28–29
  shift from adult to child focus, 16
  shift from closed to open, 17
Adoption triad
  defined, 12
  integration with professional services, 28–29
Adoptive parents
  adaptive grieving, 78
  and denial, 97
  and denial of difference, 5
  and family dysfunction, 97
  "as if" syndrome, 9–10
  case studies, 78–79, 80–81, 83
  infertility, 70
  intervention, guidelines for, 83
  issues of adolescence, 79
  issues of adulthood, 81
  issues of latency period, 77
  issues of toddler and preschool period, 75
  mourning loss of a child, 70

Subject Index

motivation to adopt, 71
placement of child in adoptive home, 73
pre adoptive period, 69
preparation for adoption, 71
psychological relationships with birth parents, 11
responding to adoptee's questions about adoption, 77–78
tasks of parenthood, 69–84
telling the child about adoption, 75–77, 87, 89
American Adoption Congress (AAC), 6, 43
Artificial Insemination by Donor (AID)
and betrayal of trust, 115
and secrecy, 113–114
and subterfuge, 115
case examples, 115
clinical issues, 115
defined, 115
genetic ties and family imbalance, 115–116
identity issues, 113–114
incidence of, 113
interventions, 116
Assertiveness Training, 40
Assessment
and Attention Deficit Disorder, 38
intake process, 34
of adoptive children, 38–39
of clients, 33–38
taking a personal history, 34–36
use of developmental information, 36
use of graphic representation, 37–38
use of normative data, 36
use of psychometric tests, 36
Association for Relinquishing Mothers (ARMS), 44, 64
Attachment work, 104
Australian
self-help groups, 43–44

Birth parents
and self-esteem, 60
case studies, 51–53, 56, 67
common trigger events, 58–60
decision to relinquish, 49
effects of relinquishment, 50
fantasies, 11
grief reactions 53, 59–60
guiding principles for therapy with, 68
immediate post-relinquish period, 53–54
incidence of, 48
intervention, 54, 61–67
post-relinquishment problems, 45, 58–61
searching, 61
services during the decision making period, 50
services during the post-relinquishment period, 56

Case management, 14
Case studies
adoptee, 87–89, 95–96
adoptive parents, 78–79, 80–81, 83
artificial insemination by donor (AID), 115
birth parents, 51–53, 56, 67
transracial adoption, 110–111
Clinical issues, 30–38
common clinical issues, 4–5, 31
defined, 30
fundamental concepts, 31
in AID and surrogacy, 115–116
in special needs adoption, 101
in surrogacy, 116–117
Concerned United Birthparents (CUB), 43, 64

Denial, 90
letting go of, 90–92, 97
Disruption, 105

Explaining adoption
and the childs understanding of, 87–89
process of, 76–77
therapeutic support for, 77
to the adopted child, 77–79
Extended adoption family, 1–2
and the search, 12
defined, 12

Family therapy, 42

Graphic representation
defined, 37
Eco-Map, 37
Famograph, 37
Geneogram, 37
Grief
and mourning loss of a child, 54–55
and relinquishment, 53
as a common issue, 31
and suicide, 54
and substance abuse, 54
reaction of birth parents, 54, 59–60
work
defined, 39
with adoptive parents, 70
with birth parents, 62

Subject Index

with children, 103
Guided fantasy, 41–42
Guilt
 and shame, 31
Guidelines
 for client assessment, 32–38
 for effective therapy, 31–32
 for self-assessment, 32–33
 for therapy with birth parents, 68

History of adoption, 15
 pre-modern period, 15
 twentieth century, 16–18
History taking
 in client assessment, 34–35
Home work assignments, 41–42

Identity, 89–90
Infertility
 and mourning, 69–71
 anger over, 70
 coping with, 70
Intake process, 34–36
Interventions
 goals of, 39
 in open adoption, 107
 in surrogacy, 117–118
 in transracial adoption, 112–113
 systemic, 13
 with adoptees, 97–98
 with adoptive parents, 72–73, 77, 80–81, 83–84
 with Artificial Insemination by Donor, 116
 with birth parents, 54–56, 61–68
International Soundex Reunion Registry (ISSR), 6, 43, 93

Jigsaw, 6
 groups in Australia and New Zealand, 44
Journal writing, 41

Legislation, 7
 and adoption laws, 16
 lobbying, 14
Life story book, 103
 in open adoption, 107
Life course developmental perspective
 and surrogate mothers, 114
 defined, xv, 7–8
 relevance to post-adoption services, 8
 social history perspective, 9

Literature and research
 contribution of, 18
Loss
 as a common issue, 31, 85

Model Statement of Post-Legal Adoption Practice, 23

National Organization for the Reunion of Child and Parent (N.O.R.C.A.P.), 44–45
New Zealand
 self-help groups, 44
North American Council on Adoptable Children (NACAC), 43

Open adoption
 clinical issues, 106–107
 defined, 7, 12, 18, 105–106
 interventions, 107
OURS, Inc., 43
 transracial, 112

Private adoption, 18
Post-adoption services
 defined, 26
 delivery of, 22–29
 financing of, 27–28
 for the adoption community, 23
 for the extended adoption family, 22–23
 integration of, 28
 need for, 22
 rationale for, 22
 training for, 27
Pregnancy counseling
 guidelines for, 50–51
Professional post-adoption services, 26–29
Projective techniques, 41
Psychometric tests
 in client assessment, 36–37

Relinquishment of a child, 53, 54
 as a secret, 66
 case studies, 51–53, 56, 57
 difficulties in discussing, 60–61
 difficulties resulting from, 50–54
 guidelines for decision making, 51
 need to reconstruct events, 62–63
 post-relinquishment issues, 56–68
 trigger events for a crisis, 58–61
Readings, 45–47
Referrals to self-help groups, 43–45
Resolve, Inc., 43, 73

Reunion
  between adoptee and birth parents, 94–96
  process, 91–96
Role handicap
  and adoptive parents, 73–74
Role play, 40

Search
  and reunion, 91–96
  as letting go of denial, 92–93
  and transracial adoption, 112
  by adoptees, 91–96
  by birth mothers, 7, 61
  case example, 95–96
  decision to, 91
  for missing family members, 12
  motivation to, 92
  process of, 93, 94
  stages of, 94
Secrecy, 3, 5, 9
  effects of, 10
  lifetime of, 5
  negative effects for birth parents, 66
Self-assessment
  guidelines for the therapist, 32
Self-help and support groups
  adoptee groups, 25
  adoption triad groups, 25
  adoptive parent groups, 25
  birth parent groups, 24
  defined, 23, 24
  in Australia, 43–44
  in New Zealand, 44
  in the United Kingdom, 44–45
  in the United States, 43
  membership by professionals, 33
  role of, 2
  value in transracial adoption, 104
  value of adoptee groups, 98
Social history perspective
  defined, 9
Special needs adoption
  clinical issues, 101
  defined, 100
  interventions, 103–105
Surrogacy, 116–118

and baby selling, 114
and surrogate motherhood, 113–114
clinical issues, 116
effect on surrogate mother, 114
interventions, 117
issues in, 113–114

"Telling the story"
  value for birth parents, 57–58, 66
  value for adoptees, 35, 98
Therapeutic interventions, 38
  assertiveness training, 40
  counseling, 39
  family therapy, 42
  goals of, 39
  grief work, 39
  guided fantasy, 39
  homework assignments, 41
  journal writing, 37
  nonverbal therapies, 41
  problem solving and conflict resolution, 39
  projective techniques, 39
  self-help groups, 42
  therapeutic support groups, 42
  therapeutic techniques, 39
Traditional adoption family
  and secrecy, 9
  defined, 9
Transracial adoption, 107–113
  case example, 110–111
  clinical issues, 111–112
  defined, 108
  interventions, 112–113
  role of adoptive parents, 1–9

United Kingdom
  self-help groups, 44–45

Workshops
  on "Healing Ourselves" for birth mothers, 66
  on transracial adoption, 112

About the Authors

Robin C. Winkler received his doctorate from the University of New South Wales in 1970. He held several visiting professor positions at Stanford University in California, Texas A & M, and the University of Thessoloniki in Greece. While an associate professor at the University of Western Australia he established and directed the Adoption Research and Counseling Service. He later became the founding chair of the Western Australia Committee on Adoption and Alternative Families. He died in November 1986.

Dirck W. Brown is the founder and first executive director of the Post Adoption Center for Education and Research (PACER) in Palo Alta, CA. He is now a therapist in Orient, NY, and continues his work on adoption through writing, conducting conferences and workshops and serving on the board of directors of the American Adoption Congress.

Margaret van Keppel served on the staff of the University of Western Australia's Adoption Research and Counseling Service, and is now at Centrecare Marriage and Family Service in Perth, Australia. Her national research study with Robin Winkler, "Relinquishing Mothers in Adoption; Their Long Term Adjustment," was published by the Australian Institute of Family Studies in 1984. Two years later she received the West Australian Women's Fellowship enabling her to travel abroad to study post-adoption services.

Amy Blanchard is a clinical psychologist in private practice in San Jose, California. She has served on the board of directors of PACER and has a special interest in clinical work with members of the adoption community. Her dissertation, "Birth Mothers Who Search: An Exploratory Study," substantially extended our knowledge base of the birth mother experience and motivation to search.

Psychology Practitioner Guidebooks

Editors
Arnold P. Goldstein, Syracuse University
Leonard Krasner, Stanford University & SUNY at Stony Brook
Sol. L. Garfield, Washington University in St. Louis

Elsie M. Pinkston & Nathan L. Linsk — CARE OF THE ELDERLY: A Family Approach

Donald Meichenbaum — STRESS INOCULATION TRAINING

Sebastiano Santostefano — COGNITIVE CONTROL THERAPY WITH CHILDREN AND ADOLESCENTS

Lillie Weiss, Melanie Katzman & Sharlene Wolchik — TREATING BULIMIA: A Psychoeducational Approach

Edward B. Blanchard & Frank Andrasik — MANAGEMENT OF CHRONIC HEADACHES: A Psychological Approach

Raymond G. Romanczyk — CLINICAL UTILIZATION OF MICRO-COMPUTER TECHNOLOGY

Philip H. Bornstein & Marcy T. Bornstein — MARITAL THERAPY: A Behavioral-Communications Approach

Michael T. Nietzel & Ronald C. Dillehay — PSYCHOLOGICAL CONSULTATION IN THE COURTROOM

Elizabeth B. Yost, Larry E. Beutler, M. Anne Corbishley & James R. Allender

— GROUP COGNITIVE THERAPY: A Treatment Method for Depressed Older Adults

Lillie Weiss — DREAM ANALYSIS IN PSYCHOTHERAPY

Edward A. Kirby & Liam K. Grimley — UNDERSTANDING AND TREATING ATTENTION DEFICIT DISORDER

Jon Eisenson — LANGUAGE AND SPEECH DISORDERS IN CHILDREN

Eva L. Feindler & Randolph B. Ecton — ADOLESCENT ANGER CONTROL: Cognitive-Behavioral Techniques

Michael C. Roberts — PEDIATRIC PSYCHOLOGY: Psychological Interventions and Strategies for Pediatric Problems

Daniel S. Kirschenbaum, William G. Johnson & Peter M. Stalonas, Jr. — TREATING CHILDHOOD AND ADOLESCENT OBESITY

W. Stewart Agras — EATING DISORDERS: Management of Obesity, Bulimia and Anorexia Nervosa

Ian H. Gotlib & Catherine A. Colby — TREATMENT OF DEPRESSION: An Interpersonal Systems Approach

Walter B. Pryzwansky & Robert N. Wendt — PSYCHOLOGY AS A PROFESSION: Foundations of Practice

Cynthia D. Belar, William W. Deardorff & Karen E. Kelly — THE PRACTICE OF CLINICAL HEALTH PSYCHOLOGY

Paul Karoly & Mark P. Jensen — MULTIMETHOD ASSESSMENT OF CHRONIC PAIN

William L. Golden, E. Thomas Dowd & Fred Friedberg — HYPNOTHERAPY: A Modern Approach

Patricia Lacks — BEHAVIORAL TREATMENT FOR PERSISTENT INSOMNIA

Arnold P. Goldstein & Harold Keller — AGGRESSIVE BEHAVIOR: Assessment and Intervention

C. Eugene Walker, Barbara L. Bonner & Keith L. Kaufman — THE PHYSICALLY AND SEXUALLY ABUSED CHILD: Evaluation and Treatment

Robert E. Becker, Richard G. Heimberg & Alan S. Bellack — SOCIAL SKILLS TRAINING TREATMENT FOR DEPRESSION

Richard F. Dangel & Richard A. Polster — TEACHING CHILD MANAGEMENT SKILLS

Albert Ellis, John F. McInerney, Raymond DiGiuseppe & Raymond Yeager — RATIONAL-EMOTIVE THERAPY WITH ALCOHOLICS AND SUBSTANCE ABUSERS

Johnny L. Matson & Thomas H. Ollendick — ENHANCING CHILDREN'S SOCIAL SKILLS: Assessment and Training

Edward B. Blanchard, John E. Martin & Patricia M. Dubbert — NON-DRUG TREATMENTS FOR ESSENTIAL HYPERTENSION

Samuel M. Turner & Deborah C. Beidel — TREATING OBSESSIVE-COMPULSIVE DISORDER

Alice W. Pope, Susan M. McHale & W. Edward Craighead — SELF-ESTEEM ENHANCEMENT WITH CHILDREN AND ADOLESCENTS

Jean E. Rhodes & Leonard A. Jason — PREVENTING SUBSTANCE ABUSE AMONG CHILDREN AND ADOLESCENTS

Gerald D. Oster, Janice E. Caro, Daniel R. Eagen & Margaret A. Lillo — ASSESSING ADOLESCENTS

Robin C. Winkler, Dirck W. Brown, Margaret van Keppel & Amy Blanchard — CLINICAL PRACTICE IN ADOPTION